D1415078

Praise for *Leadership Sustainability*

"*Leadership Sustainability* offers a unique perspective on seven disciplines that truly impact leadership. The tools and examples outlined in this book will enable emergent leaders to grow and existing leaders to sharpen their skills. All leaders can benefit from a reminder of why and how to lead, and this model provides very clear guidance. Excellent work by Dave Ulrich and Norm Smallwood."

—Allen B. Alexander, Chairman and CEO, Savage Companies

"Evidence shows that on average one of every two individuals holding a position of leadership fail—an unacceptable record. The usual bromides found in most books on leadership have not helped with this problem. The seven leadership disciplines provided by Ulrich and Smallwood are the significantly unique features and contributions of this book. Finally, we have two scholar-practitioners who have correctly addressed *the* issues—they are less about the leader and more about leadership, and they are about proper execution that leads to sustainability."

—W. Warner Burke, Ph.D., Edward Lee Thorndike Professor of Psychology and Education, Teachers College, Columbia University

"Borrowing from Britney Spears, "Oops, they've done it again." It seems every time we think we know everything we need to know from their last book, then they do it again. Are we ever going to get any rest? Now we have to memorize the seven disciplines and much more importantly learn how to apply them in our lives and to the leaders we serve. They are very right, again. This book will add value to any manager or leader. Again, it keeps adding to the mosaic of leadership. Always right. Always surprisingly simple. Always doable. Always a 'have-to-read.'"

—Bob Eichinger, retired, former Vice Chairman of KornFerry International and CEO and cofounder of Lominger Limited Inc.

"Sustainability is *the* greatest challenge in leadership development. Dave and Norm have done the best work I have ever seen in tackling this challenge! While some books can help you *become* a great leader, this book can help you *remain* a great leader! While good leaders understand the practice of leadership, great leaders practice their understanding of leadership. *Leadership Sustainability* shows you how!"

—*Marshall Goldsmith, author of New York Times bestsellers MOJO and What Got You Here Won't Get You There, World's #1 Leadership Thinker (Thinkers50 global survey, sponsored by Harvard Business Review).*

"Leaders all over the world will celebrate Dave's and Norm's powerful new gift: the concept of *Leadership Sustainability*, and its seven disciplines. Leaders across the sectors and at every level will find the new Ulrich-Smallwood book the indispensable companion for their leadership journey."

—*Frances Hesselbein, President and CEO, The Frances Hesselbein Leadership Institute*

"Short-term impact by leaders is not easy but it is common. For those aspiring to achieve that rare leadership feat of effecting genuine, long-term change and success, the insights of Ulrich and Smallwood are not to be missed!"

—*Matthew S. Holland, President, Utah Valley University*

"In our jam-packed over-burdened world, I loved seeing a leadership book with seven one-word chapter headings as the "meat!" Each one spoke to me as being essential to the leadership equation yet not quite fleshed out in any other book. They streamline the complexity of their subject and provide critical how-tos! All you have to do to be hooked is to read the opening paragraph in the preface of this book. (How sad is that?) These authors call it as they see it and win the rights to do just that because of their deep and wide experience in the corporate leadership arena. I resonated particularly with the authors' belief that good leaders build future leaders and that they leave their legacy with the teams of people who they challenge, nurture, and grow."

—*Beverly Kaye, founder, Chair of the Board: Career Systems International coauthor: Help Them Grow or Watch Them Go: Career Conversations Employees Want*

"A must read for any leader who is genuinely interested in making real improvements in his/her leadership in a manner which is observable, sustainable, and for the long-term good for the organization."

—*Peck Kem Low, Divisional Director, National HR, Singapore Ministry of Manpower*

"Leadership can be instinctive; execution of those instincts takes discipline and maniacal execution. Read on—you'll learn!!"

—Randy MacDonald, Senior Vice President, Human Resources, IBM

"The road to derailment is paved with good intentions. Who among us has not recognized something about ourselves that gets in our way— reducing our effectiveness, blocking promotion, eroding relationships? And who among us has at the same time, and with the best of intentions, failed to make the changes we knew we needed to make? Dave Ulrich and Norm Smallwood, drawing on many years of experience analyzing leadership in the world's most admired companies, have directly confronted that gap and provide both an in-depth understanding of why we often fall short and a set of tools for getting on with it. After reading this book you'll have no excuses."

—Morgan W. McCall, Jr., Professor, Marshall School of Business,
University of Southern California (and author of High Flyers:
Developing the Next Generation of Leaders)

"In *Leadership Sustainability*, Ulrich and Smallwood do a great job about teaching leaders not just what to do, but how to make sure that they do it. The book's global appeal comes from cases and examples around the world of leaders who know what to do and now have the disciplines to do it. It will become the standard template for action planning out of coaching, training, development, 360, and other performance improvement efforts. The ideas in the book are insightful, specific, and actionable. Using these ideas will help any good leader become better."

—Gina Qiao 乔健, SVP Human Resources, Lenovo

"Some time ago, I was seated in a large conference room with at least 1,000 other people, listening to Dave Ulrich. Suddenly he spotted me and asked, 'Ken, what do you consider to be *the single most important issue* in leadership today?' My answer: **leadership sustainability**. Later, Dave and Norm Smallwood not only addressed this mega-issue but nailed it: This is the *definitive work* on the matter and an *instant classic* in the field."

—Ken Shelton, editor/CEO, Leadership Excellence

"Those who want to know Why, What, and How of Leadership Sustainability, this book is a must read! Dave and Norm have given the key to the readers to find direction and probable answers within, to the questions they always had in their minds. Finish what you start is one of the key messages of the book. Live examples in the book help you to navigate better in your day-to-day life. I am sure readers will profit their mind and organization!"

—Dhananjay Singh, Executive Director, National HRD Network

"Finally, a 'how to' book that is grounded in the real-world dynamics of leading organizations! Unlike most others, this book unfolds as if there were a leadership coach at your side giving you useable counsel and tools to actually create your own self-sustaining leadership advantage."

—Dixon Thayer, CEO, HealthNEXT

"No leadership skill matters if it cannot actually be implemented and sustained. In this timely, practical, and lucid book, veteran leadership experts Dave Ulrich and Norm Smallwood show us how to successfully influence others by influencing ourselves first. I recommend it highly!"

—William Ury, coauthor of Getting to YES and
author of The Power of a Positive No.

"There's no doubt that *Leadership Sustainability* will hold a reserved spot on bookshelves in business leaders' offices the world over—that is, when it is not being referred to. Ulrich and Smallwood's work helps ensure we understand the strategies behind sustained leadership agent. They understand that two of the keys to success are disciplined continuity and sustainability—which constitute a required core competency among leadership agents. Their newest book is a thoughtful and practical approach to accomplishing that."

—Kathleen Wilson-Thompson, Chief Human
Resources Officer, Walgreen Co.

LEADERSHIP SUSTAINABILITY

Seven Disciplines to Achieve
the Changes Great Leaders
Know They Must Make

Dave Ulrich
Norm Smallwood

New York   Chicago   San Francisco   Lisbon   London
Madrid   Mexico City   Milan   New Delhi   San Juan
Seoul   Singapore   Sydney   Toronto

1 2 3 4 5 6 7 8 9 0   DOC/DOC   1 9 8 7 6 5 4 3

ISBN: 978-0-07-180852-1
MHID: 0-07-180852-3

e-ISBN: 978-0-07-180853-8
e-MHID: 0-07-180853-1

Library of Congress Cataloging-in-Publication Data

Ulrich, David.
    Leadership sustainability : seven disciplines to achieve the changes great leaders know they must make / by Dave Ulrich and Norm Smallwood. — 1 Edition.
    pages   cm
    ISBN-13: 978-0-07-180852-1 (alk. paper)
    ISBN-10: 0-07-180852-3 (alk. paper)
    1. Leadership.   I. Smallwood, W. Norman.   II. Title.
    HD57.7.U45797 2013
    658.4'092—dc23   2012042817

McGraw-Hill books are available at special quantity discounts to use as premiums and sales promotions, or for use in corporate training programs. To contact a representative, please e-mail us at bulksales@mcgraw-hill.com.

This book is printed on acid-free paper.

*To our grandchildren who embody our
hope for a sustainable future*

CONTENTS

PREFACE

Most good leaders want and try to become better. Around the world today, and every day of the year, thousands of leaders will attend leadership training to glean insights into how to lead better. Thousands will receive performance reviews with individual development plans on how to improve. Thousands will receive coaching with recommendations on how to change their behavior so as to deliver better results in better ways. Thousands will complete a 360-degree feedback process with data on how they are seen by others. At the end of the training, performance development, coaching, and 360-degree feedback, most of these leaders will resolve to use their new insights to become more effective. Unfortunately, few of them will implement these good intentions.

Leaders do not always accomplish what they intend or finish what they start. At the end of every leadership improvement effort, participants need the discipline to do what they desire and to turn their aspirations into actions. This book has a very simple purpose: to help leaders sustain the changes that they know they should make—that is, to support *leadership sustainability.*

Leadership sustainability is a concept with parallels in environmental sustainability, which has come to mean shaping an organization's culture and all its actions to enhance its reputation as a responsible member of its community and custodian of the world's resources. Leadership sustainability begins with recognition that what matters most is the impact of the leader's actions on others—not just the actions themselves or the rationale behind them. Leadership sustainability has to show up not only in personal intentions but also in observable behaviors.

Audience

Given our simple aim to help leaders sustain the changes they know they should make, who are we writing for here?

- *Any leader who wants to be better and who knows what to do to improve but struggles to make it last.*
- *Everyone charged with developing future leaders.* This includes line managers who have primary responsibility for building the next generation of leaders within their organizations, and it also includes learning and training specialists whose primary task is to design and deliver training that has an impact. Leaders who develop future leaders make sure that desired improvements happen.
- *Human resources (HR) professionals, coaches, and peers whose work includes helping leaders sustain desired changes.* To be a leader-maker means not only helping leaders figure out why they should change and what they should change but also helping them build discipline on how to make the change last.

Structure of the Book

We've spent years researching and then applying our ideas about why leadership is important and what good leadership looks like. Yet, as we work with leaders around the world, we still see a gap between what people know they should do and what gets done. In part, the problem is that much information is available, across such a variety of academic fields, that it is easy to become confused about what really works, and this concept clutter is not helpful to leaders who want to improve. So our work for this book synthesizes research from multiple fields—business, psychology, sociology, and so on—into an integrated set of disciplines that can make the difference between good intentions and effective action.

Background

Chapter 1 goes into more depth on the need for leadership sustainability and explores how it complements our journey of leadership insights. We have found that leadership development matters, and personal change is not easy, even with coaching. In addition, developing leadership capability (the capability to build future leaders) matters even more than developing individual competence. This chapter sets the stage for the discussion of the seven disciplines, each of which forms the basis for one of the following chapters:

- Simplicity
- Time
- Accountability
- Resources
- Tracking
- Melioration
- Emotion

Simplicity

Chapter 2 addresses the importance of focusing on the key behaviors that will make the most difference to the most important issues. The world is increasingly complex as technology makes global events local news. Leaders have to cope with complexity not only in the world around them but also in their personal leadership style. Most leaders create extensive to-do lists of things they should change—but they get overwhelmed when they try to change them all at once. Leadership sustainability requires finding simplicity in the face of complexity and replacing concept clutter with simple resolve. It entails prioritizing the behaviors that matter most, shifting from analytics with data to action with determination, framing complex phenomena into simple patterns, and sequencing change.

Time

Chapter 3 focuses on leaders passing the calendar test. It takes up the question of the allocation of days, hours, and moments. We often ask leaders we coach to tell us their priorities, which most can do. Then we ask them to review their calendar for the last 30 or 90 days and show us how much time they spent on these priorities—an exercise that often reveals unnerving gaps between intention and reality. Effective leaders build their desired behaviors into their calendars, and this shows up in how they spend their time. Employees attend to what they see leaders do far more than to what they hear them say. Leadership sustainability shows up in who we spend time with, what issues we spend time on, where we spend our time, and how we spend our time. When leaders invest their time as carefully as their money, they are more likely to make change happen.

Accountability

Chapter 4 discusses the clear benefits of accepting responsibility and holding yourself and others accountable for keeping promises. A cycle of cynicism occurs when leaders announce wonderful aspirations (e.g., vision, mission, and strategy statements) but fail to deliver. Over time, this cycle breaks down trust and erodes commitment. Leadership sustainability requires leaders to take personal responsibility for making sure that they do what they say. Accountability also increases when leaders expect and accept personal commitments from others and follow up on those commitments. Over time, leadership is sustainable when the leader's agenda becomes the personal agenda of others.

Resources

Chapter 5 focuses on the specific resources of coaching and HR infrastructure that leaders can enlist to support their desired changes and build an infrastructure of sustainability. We have found that a mix of self-coaching, expert coaching, peer coaching, and boss coaching can be woven together to resource sustained change. HR practices can define and create an organization's culture. Selection, promotion, career development, succession planning, performance review, and communication policies can be aligned with organization design to support leadership change.

Tracking

Chapter 6 returns to some wise old sayings: You get what you inspect and not what you expect; you do what you are rewarded for (and so does everyone else); and you shouldn't reward one thing while hoping for something different. Leaders must measure their behaviors and results in specific ways. Unless desired leadership behaviors and changes are translated into specific actions, quantified, and tracked, they are nice to contemplate but not likely to get done. Effective metrics for leadership behavior need to be transparent, easy to measure, timely, and tied to consequences. Leadership sustainability can be woven into existing scorecards and even become its own scorecard to ensure that leaders monitor how they are doing.

Melioration

Chapter 7 introduces a new term for actions and attitudes designed to make things better. Leaders *meliorate* when they improve by learning from mistakes and failures and demonstrate resilience. Change is not linear. We don't often start at point *A* and end up in a logical and smooth progression at point Z. Most of the time, we try, fail (or succeed), try again, fail again, and so forth. When we learn from each attempt, the outcomes we intend will eventually come to pass. Leadership sustainability requires that leaders master the principles of learning: to experiment frequently, to reflect always, to become resilient, to face failure, to not be calloused to success, and to improvise continually.

Emotion

Chapter 8 addresses the value of emotion, pointing out that leaders who sustain change have a personal passion for the changes they need to make. Sustained change is a matter of the heart as well as the head; it needs a strong emotional agenda and not simply an intellectual agenda, however logical and cogent it may be. Action without passion will not long endure, nor will passion without action. Leaders ensure emotion by drawing on their deeper values and finding meaning in the work they do. Leadership sustainability occurs when leaders not only know but also feel what they should do to improve. This passion increases when leaders see their desired changes as part of their personal identity and purpose, when their changes will shape their relationships with others, and when their changes will shift the culture of their work setting.

Conclusion

Chapter 9 introduces an application audit to apply these disciplines to sustain their leadership progress. Our hope is that leaders who want to make something happen by changing their behavior or the behavior of others will find the application audit introduced in this chapter a practical tool to ensure that desired changes are actually introduced—and then stick.

We invite you to join us on our journey to develop individual leaders and to build better organization leadership capability in your organization. Our website offers specific tools and examples of sustainable success: www.leadershipsustainability.com.

ACKNOWLEDGMENTS

Every book we write is a labor of love … and late nights, writer's block, word amnesia, concept clutter, and idea phobia. We ground our work in the phenomenon we study by listening diligently to challenges we experience in working with and observing clients. We try to find unique and creative ways to solve unrecognized challenges. In doing this work, we need to acknowledge our many thought partners. This includes our clients who allow us to coach, consult, and co-learn. Without their candor and openness, we would not recognize their unsolved challenges. We value the leaders who have shared their personal stories.

We appreciate others who play in our sandbox and inform our thinking, in the case of leadership sustainability, these colleagues include: Dick Beatty, Wayne Brockbank, Ram Charan, Sean Covey, Jeff Dyer, Bob Eichinger, Tammy Erickson, Marshall Goldsmith, Lynda Gratton, Gary Hamel, Beverly Kay, John Kotter, Ed Lawler, Morgan McCall, Kerry Patterson, Jeff Pfeffer, Bonner Ritchie, Bob Sutton, Bill Ury, and Jon Younger. We especially appreciate Hilary Powers, our "write knight," who has edited many of our books and continues to turn our abstract ideas into wonderful words. Thanks also to Knox Huston at McGraw-Hill who not only edits but also guides us.

We are very grateful to our colleagues at the RBL Group who offer enormous support. The team of Erin Burns, Justin Britton, Ryan Lusvardi, Justin Hyatt, and Elisa Visick have worked on the app, the website, and other marketing support for this book. We particularly acknowledge client sponsors of the RBL Institute and our Institute management team. We recognize the unique support of Ginger Bitter and Lisa Griep who coordinate our schedules and lives. And, most important, we appreciate beyond words the support and undeserved patience of our wives, Wendy and Tricia, who sacrifice more than we deserve.

CHAPTER 1

DO NOT WALK HOME 1

Imagine this: *A group of turkeys attend a two-day training program to learn how to fly. They learn the principles of aerodynamics, and they practice flying in the morning, afternoon, and evening. They learn to fly with the wind and against it, over mountains and plains, and together and solo. At the end of the two days, they all walk home.*

Real-World Leadership Development

This old sketch captures current reality. Most good leaders make earnest attempts to become better through coaching, individual development plans, training, and performance improvement plans. Through each of these efforts, leaders learn what to do to be more effective—and it's not cheap. An estimated $60 to $80 billion is spent annually on only training in the United States alone.[1] To imagine this scale, if this money represented the revenues of one firm, it would rank between twenty-fifth (Procter & Gamble) and forty-first (Dell) on the Fortune 500. Some have suggested that training costs are about 2.0 to 2.5 percent of payroll, that the spend per learner is between $1,000 and $1,200 per year, and that employees receive about 40 hours of training per year.[2] And these are direct costs for training, not including opportunity time and salary of those who attend.

About 20 percent of all training dollars go for leadership development and management and supervisory training, making this the largest single area of investment. Debate rages about how much of what is taught in leadership courses actually transfers to leadership practice.

Some have suggested that knowledge transfer is as low as 10 percent.[3] Other studies show the number closer to 60 percent.[4] We estimate that 20 to 30 percent of ideas learned in leadership training turn into practice. Whichever of these statistics you believe, it is clear that the investment in leadership improvement through training (as well as coaching, performance management, and individual development plans as well) is not having the impact it could or should.

These investments in leadership improvement come as a response to persistent calls for improving the quality of leadership. In many surveys of senior executives, leadership has been and remains a top priority. In a Duke study of C-suite executives, leadership development is the number two challenge facing organizations.[5] In our "Top Companies for Leadership" research, we found that companies that invested in leadership had much higher business performance than those that didn't.[6] McKinsey partnered with Egon Zehnder to study growth performance of more than 700 companies and found that leadership quality is "critical to growth" and that most companies do not have enough high-quality executives.[7] The Boston Consulting Group also found that improving leadership development was a top priority from a recent survey of 2,039 business leaders.[8]

Similar results could be shared for performance management, coaching, and 360-degree feedback. While leadership matters and a lot of money is spent on improving leadership, it is not clear that these investments build lasting value. Unless and until leadership insight turns into leadership action, efforts to increase leadership quality amount to flying lessons for the confirmed pedestrian.

The Personal Case

Most of us have personal habits we would like to change. Most leaders have behaviors that they would like to change. Dan, a leader we coached, was head of finance at his company.[9] He had exceptional technical skills, having spent 25 years moving up the organization and gaining certification by all the right professional associations. No one doubted his technical ability. He was well liked by his team and respected throughout the organization for his technical insights. But he had a leadership flaw.

He talked too much.

In personal interchanges, he dominated the conversation, speaking 70 to 80 percent of the time. In professional team meetings, he would control and dominate every meeting. When asked questions by bosses, peers, or subordinates, he would ramble over the whole topic instead of providing the specific information needed.

We were asked to coach him by those in the company who sincerely wanted him to succeed. He recognized that he had a tendency to be verbose. He knew that this tendency got him in trouble. He respected others and valued his team, but he just could not help himself when he spoke. We collected feedback on his behavior, shared with him the unintended consequences of his verbosity, agreed to an action plan to change the behavior, and followed up regularly. But his behavior did not change. He wanted to be a good leader, he knew what to do to be a better leader, but he could not sustain his desired change.

The Company Case

Individuals need discipline to turn leadership aspirations to actions, and so do companies. We were asked to help a company prepare its leaders to become better strategists. The company was not able to anticipate changing market trends, to articulate a clear and simple vision for its future, or to increase its customer-service scores. We worked with the senior line managers and strategic planning experts to map out what the company had done with their strategic work. We prepared leadership training where leaders would learn how to define market trends, where they would practice applying principles of strategic clarity to their vision and mission, and where they would define and practice actions to increase customer share. For a short period, the models and frameworks took hold. The company did market position statements, it crafted a strategic vision, and it put in place customer-service programs. After about six months, though, many of these initiatives faded, and people fell back into their previous practices. We had covered the traditional knowledge-transfer checklist, but somehow it did not stick.

The Implications

Leaders matter. No one doubts that leaders make a difference in company results. Evidence proves it, and personal experience validates it.

Leadership matters more. An individual leader can make a lot of noise and raise the bar on expectations, but collective leadership binds leaders at all levels of the organization to shared and sustainable actions.

Leadership development matters. As the world changes, the skills of leaders must evolve. Marshall Goldsmith eloquently says, "What got you here won't get you there." Leaders derail when they fail to learn and grow with their markets and business. Unfortunately, in many development experiences, even when leaders learn they do not change enough to do things differently.

Personal change is not easy to sustain. Most of us know one or two things we want to change about ourselves (e.g., more caring for loved ones, more patience, more healthy eating, more regular exercise, more sleep, more balance in our lives, more financial responsibility). But knowing what to do does not mean we do it. Often when we attempt to make personal improvements, recidivism kicks in and bad habits persist. Consider the following statistics[10]:

- Ninety-eight percent of us fail at keeping New Year's resolutions to change bad habits.

- Seventy percent of Americans who pay off credit-card debt with a home-equity loan end up with the same or higher debt in two years.
- Americans spend $40 billion a year on diets, but 19 out of 20 lose nothing but their money.
- Marriage counseling saves fewer than one in five couples on the brink of divorce.

Change through coaching, transfer from training to practice, or individual development plans is also very difficult. Even tailored performance management systems rarely make much difference. Like Dan, the executive with the unrestrainable tongue, most leaders find that knowing is not doing, and the challenge is often less what to do and more how to build the discipline to sustain it. Consider some additional statistics:

- A VitalSmarts study found that 73 percent of employees have been in circumstances where they knew they needed to change to keep their job or to get ahead yet were unable to successfully change their habits.
- Knowledge Advisors discovered that 76 percent of all the training managers who responded to a survey indicated that training is a key organization tool, but 9 percent of learners actually apply what they learn with positive results. In addition, 76 percent indicated that learners apply 50 percent or less of what they learn.
- McKinsey found that only 30 percent of major initiatives succeed —and that proportion drops to 19 percent for culture-change initiatives. The conclusion: "The crucial issue is how the change is accomplished, not so much what the change is."

Ultimately, as individual leaders improve, the companies where they work also improve, becoming more able to sustain the transformations they intend. So the ideas in this book will help leaders to accomplish the corporate transformations they regard as necessary.

Leadership Sustainability

We call this work *leadership sustainability*. The term draws logic and insight from the field of environmental sustainability, which has evolved from isolated corporate social responsibility programs to a broad focus on changing a culture to include patterns of action that enhance external reputation.

The concept of environmental sustainability began by considering the context of the organization. The concept of leadership sustainability begins with recognition that what matters is the impact of the leader's actions on others—not just what the leader does or means to do. This addresses the natural human tendency to judge ourselves by our intentions, whereas others judge us (and we judge others) by behavior. Leadership sustainability has to show up not only in personal intentions but also in observable behavior.

Environmental sustainability is about caring for the earth's resources by reducing our demand for things that cannot be replaced and our output of harmful things that will not go away. Leadership sustainability is about caring for the organization's resources by adapting and changing leadership patterns so that they are consistent with shifting requirements. Environmental sustainability has shifted to a social agenda that involves giving back to the community through corporate social responsibility initiatives. Leadership sustainability occurs when leaders take personal responsibility for ensuring that they do what they say they will do, with beneficial results.

Environmental sustainability has further evolved to become a long-term commitment to changing the world in which we live and work and to creating a new culture inside our companies. Leadership sustainability is a lasting and durable commitment to personal change and creating a culture of leadership improvement that affects all leaders in a company. It is the next step in our journey of leadership. Table 1.1 summarizes the comparison between the two.

Table 1.1   Defining Environmental and Leadership Sustainability

Environmental Sustainability	Leadership Sustainability
Considering the context in which the organization operates	Considering the impact on all individuals affected by a leader's actions
Caring for the earth's resources and avoiding damage	Caring for the organization's resources and improving productivity
Giving back through social responsibility and conservation initiatives	Giving back by taking personal responsibility for doing what is promised
Making a long-term commitment to change the world	Making a lasting and durable commitment to personal change

Our Leadership Journey

Over the past 20 years, we have worked to help individuals be better leaders and to build better leadership capability in their organizations. Our work has followed the same process in order to turn ideas into impact. At each step of this journey, we start with a relatively simple question and then scan the latest theory, research, and practice to discover alternative ways to answer the question. Then we use principles of *taxonomy*—the science of finding patterns—to synthesize what we find into a straightforward framework or typology that captures the ideas and enhances their power.

With this taxonomic logic in mind, we believe that the challenges of leadership can be simplistically captured in three phases and questions (Table 1.2):

- *Why.* Why does leadership matter?
- *What.* What makes an effective leader?
- *How.* How do leaders sustain their desired improvements?

Table 1.2   *The Evolution of Leadership Thinking: Why and What, Now How*

Phase and Leadership Challenge	Leadership Question	Leadership Failure	Our Books on Topics
1. *Need*	*Why:* Why does leadership *matter*?	Failure of rationale. No one is making a strong case for leadership.	• *Results-Based Leadership* • *Why the Bottom Line Isn't (or How Leaders Build Value)*
2. *Vision*	*What:* What is our theory of leadership? What does it mean to be an effective leader? What are the right standards of leadership?	Failure of accuracy. Leaders and leadership are not doing the right things.	• *Leadership Code* • *Leadership Brand* • *Why of Work*
3. *Action*	*How:* How do I become a better leader? How does my organization sustain leadership by weaving it into the organization systems?	Failure of sustainability. Leaders don't finish what they start.	• *Leadership Sustainability* (this book)

In the past, we have concentrated on the first two phases, which we review briefly here. The third phase, summarized at the end of this section, is the focus of this book.

Why

Why does leadership matter? In our early work, we started with a simple insight—much of the practice of leadership was focused on individual psychological competencies. Virtually every book we could find then, and to a great extent now, was aimed at individual leader competency development (what we called the *attributes of leaders*). Popular examples:

- *Seven Habits of Highly Effective People* (and its sequels)
- *Authenticity*
- *Leadership Secrets of …* (whoever came to the would-be author's mind: Attila the Hun, Thomas Jefferson, Buddha, Santa Claus, and so on and on)
- *Emotional Intelligence*
- *Judgment*
- *The Extraordinary Leader*

In seminars we often ask, "What makes an effective leader?" The response generally covers much the same ground: setting a vision, having integrity, communicating, being bold, making things happen, and other personal attributes. Frequently, leadership development experiences are organized with a day on each attribute.

We proposed that this approach was half right. Leaders do need to have effective attributes, but leadership is also about getting results. So, in our book, *Results-Based Leadership*, we explored four results that leaders need to deliver:

- *Employee.* Leaders increase employee productivity by building competence, commitment, and contribution among the workforce.
- *Organization.* Leaders must build sustainable capabilities that shape an organization's identity.
- *Customer.* Leaders ensure customer share by creating long-term relationships that delight target customers.
- *Investor.* Leaders build intangible value (which is about 50 percent of a firm's market value) by creating investor confidence in future earnings.

We have since added a fifth:

- *Community.* Leaders establish their organization's reputation by becoming active community citizens.

It was at this time that we realized the importance of the relationship between attributes and results. Neither alone is enough—it's the virtuous cycle between them that makes all the difference, as sketched in Figure 1.1. We connect attributes and results with *so that* and *because of.* One simple application is that when a leader receives 360-degree feedback, which is about individual competencies, it is essential to pose the *so that* query. I must improve this competency *so that* I deliver a particular result to one of my stakeholders. Alternatively, another leader delivers results and should ask the *because of* question. I delivered this result *because of* this competency I have (or lack).

It is critical for leaders to know why leadership matters. Leadership is about linking attributes to results.

Figure 1.1   The virtuous cycle of attributes and results.

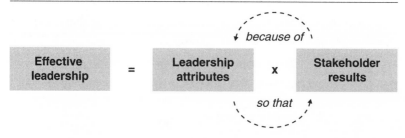

What

What makes an effective leader? If leadership matters (the *why* question), then what must leaders know and do to make that important difference? As we thought about this question, we began to focus on the importance of brand as a metaphor for defining leadership. The concept of leadership brand as a metaphor for effective leadership draws on two conceptual shifts in leadership thinking:

- *From a focus on the leader as a person to a focus on leadership as a capability within the organization.* The metaphor of brand is more about leadership than about the characteristics of individual leaders.
- *From a focus on what happens inside the leader or inside the firm to a focus on meeting customer, investor, and other external expectations.* The metaphor of brand starts from the outside and focuses clearly on business results.

This typology leads to four approaches to leadership (as outlined in Figure 1.2):

- *Competent leaders:* Determine and develop the knowledge and skills of the individual leader.
- *Leadership systems:* Align selection, development, compensation, and retention systems to reinforce desired leadership behavior.

Figure 1.2   Leadership approaches.

Outside	Celebrity leaders ⟶	Leadership brand
Inside	Competent leaders	Leadership systems
	Leader	**Leadership**

- *Celebrity leaders:* Recruit or sponsor famous leaders who are known to customers and investors and who help to draw attention and resources to the firm.
- *Leadership brand:* Develops leaders at every level who are recognized by employees as well as customers and investors for their ability to deliver results in a manner consistent with firm brand identity.

Leadership brand integrates the other three views and offers a robust definition of what makes an effective leader. It translates customer expectations into internal behaviors so that leaders ensure that employees deliver the desired customer experience whenever they touch the customer. We further found that leadership brand is made up of two elements: the code and the differentiators (Figure 1.3).

Code represents the basic requirements that every leader must possess. (To extend the product brand metaphor, these are the characteristics that a successful product offers.) *Differentiators* are those unique characteristics and behavior patterns that allow organizations to distinguish themselves in the minds of their customers.

Figure 1.3   *The two parts of leadership brand.*

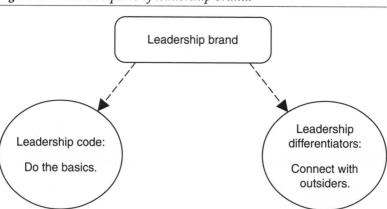

In the spirit of taxonomy, we discovered the leadership code by interviewing recognized experts in the field who had already spent years sifting through the evidence and developing their own theories. These thought leaders had each published a theory of leadership based on a long history of leadership research and empirical assessment of what makes effective leadership. Collectively, they had written more than 80 books on leadership and performed well over 2 million leadership 360-degree reviews. They are the thought leaders of this field.[11]

In our discussions with these thought leaders, we focused on two simple questions whose answers had always been elusive:

- What percentage of effective leadership is basically the same everywhere?
- If there are common rules that all leaders must master, what are they?

To the first question, the experts varied, estimating that somewhere in the range of 50 to 80 percent of leadership characteristics were shared by all effective leaders. The range is fairly broad, to be sure, but consistent. From the body of interviews we conducted, we concluded that 60 to 70 percent of leadership effectiveness is shared across the board. Synthesizing the data, the interviews, and our own research and experience, a framework emerged that we simply call the *leadership code*.

In an effort to create a useful visual aid, we have mapped out two dimensions (time and focus) and placed what we are calling *personal proficiency* (self-management) at the center as an underlying support for the other two. Figure 1.4 synthesizes the leadership code and captures the five rules of leadership that encompass the essence of leadership.

Figure 1.4   The leadership code.

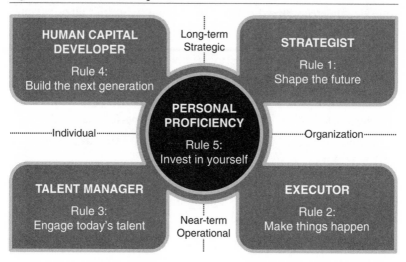

These five rules can be readily applied to any group of leaders:

Rule 1: Shape the future. Strategists answer the question, "Where are we going?" and make sure that those around them understand the direction as well. They not only envision but also create a future. The rules for strategists are about creating, defining, and delivering principles of what can be.

Rule 2: Make things happen. Executors focus on the question, "How will we make sure we get where we want to go?" Executors translate strategy into action. The rules for executors are about disciplines for getting things done and the technical expertise to get the right things done right.

Rule 3: Engage today's talent. Talent managers answer the question, "Who goes with us on our business journey?" Talent managers coach and communicate with their employees around competence (skills), commitment (engagement), and contribution (meaning). The rules for talent managers are about helping people to develop themselves for the good of the organization.

Rule 4: Build the next generation. Human capital developers answer the question, "Who stays and sustains the organization as newcomers join it?" While talent managers ensure shorter-term results through people, human capital developers ensure that the organization has the longer-term competencies required for future strategic success. Human capital developers instill rules that demonstrate a pledge to building the talent the organization will need as conditions change.

Rule 5: Invest in yourself. At the heart of the leadership code—literally and figuratively—is personal proficiency. Effective leaders cannot be reduced to what they know and do. Who they are as human beings has everything to do with how much they can accomplish with and through other people. Personally proficient leaders take care of themselves intellectually (by learning), physically (by managing their bodies and space), emotionally (by renewing themselves), socially (by connecting to others), and spiritually (by attending to personal values). Leaders who are personally proficient rule, or govern, themselves so that others willingly trust and follow them.

We have worked with these five rules of leadership over the last decade, and we can make some summary observations:

- All leaders must excel at personal proficiency. Without the foundation of trust and credibility, you cannot ask others to follow you. While individuals may have different styles (e.g., introvert or extrovert, intuitive or sensing, and so on), any individual leader must be seen as having personal proficiency to engage followers. This is probably the toughest of the five domains to train, and some individuals are naturally more capable than others.
- Effective leaders often have one towering strength. Most successful leaders have at least one of the other four roles in which they excel.

Most are personally predisposed to one of the four areas. These are the signature strengths of your leaders.

- All leaders must be at least average in all four of the outer leadership domains. It is possible to train someone to be strategic, execute, manage talent, and develop future talent. Each area includes behaviors and skills that can be identified, developed, and mastered.
- The higher up the organization leaders rise, the more they need to develop excellence across all four domains.

It is very bold to say that these five domains synthesize and summarize what makes effective leadership, but we continue to believe that these five domains represent the code—the basics of leadership.

Having identified the basics, we then wanted to explore the 30 to 40 percent of leadership brand that constitutes the differentiators. To do this, we started with being clear about customer expectations. In this work, we often begin by looking at branding efforts. We look at video, print, and Internet commercials to define what messages the organization is sending to its target customers. Once these messages are specified, we look at the leadership competence model and leadership development programs to see if they are consistent with these customer expectations. Often the message outside the organization is not consistent with the leadership theory or investment inside the organization, and excellence in the differentiators involves bringing the two into agreement.

How

How do leaders sustain their desired improvements? Most, if not all, the leaders we work with know the importance of leadership for their organization's success. Most also want to be better leaders, and this leads them to adopt personal improvement goals, to participate in training and development activities, and to invest in the leadership of others in their organization. In leadership workshops or coaching, we often start with three questions:

- On a scale of 1 (low) to 10 (high), how important is leadership for either your personal or organizational success? Most answer 8, 9, or 10.
- What specific things do you need to do to be a more effective leader? Most can quickly write down two or three desired behaviors.
- How long have you known that you should improve these behaviors? Most meekly acknowledge that they have known what to improve for 3, 6, or 12 months—or longer (decades for some).

In this simple exercise, we don't discount the *why* and *what* of leadership, but most still don't accomplish the leadership improvements to which they aspire. These improvements may come from a stronger desire to lead better or from being able to upgrade the right skills. But we believe that many leaders are at a point of diminishing returns by focusing only on the *why* and *what* of leadership. By shifting attention to the *how*, leaders emphasize finding ways to sustain desired improvements.

None of the initiatives to improve leadership (e.g., training, 360, performance management, and coaching) sufficiently transfers to practice. Well-meaning leadership training, individual development plans, coaching, or 360-degree sessions tend to be energizing events, but the energy dissipates quickly. The action planning done at the end of a leadership improvement exercise is too often an afterthought or simply disjointed activities. Today's biggest unmet challenge of leadership is not learning more about what to do, it is learning how to make sure that what is known is done. To meet this challenge, our leadership journey now turns to *how* to make leadership happen, to bring focus and discipline to action learning so that leadership aspirations turn into results. We approach this problem the same way we have approached our leadership work about *why* and *what* in the past. We began by gleaning lessons from a number of fields that bear on the challenge of leadership sustainability. We have reviewed and synthesized the literature to identify disciplines of sustainable change. These topics come from diverse literatures; in case you'd like to begin your own exploration, some exemplar books are summarized in Table 1.3.

Table 1.3   *Topics and Exemplar Books on Leadership Sustainability*

Making change happen:
- Chip Heath and Dan Heath, *Made to Stick: Why Some Ideas Survive and Others Die*
- John Norcross and Carlo DiClemente, *Changing for Good: A Revolutionary Six-Stage Program for Overcoming Bad Habits and Moving Your Life Positively Forward*
- Jeffrey Pfeffer and Robert Sutton, *The Knowing/Doing Gap*

Influence and persuasion:
- Robert Cialdini, *Influence: The Psychology of Persuasion*
- Roger Fisher, William Ury, and Bruce Patton, *Getting to Yes: Negotiating Agreement Without Giving In*

Changing habits:
- Cherry Pedrick, *The Habit Change Workbook: How to Break Bad Habits and Form Good Ones*
- M. J. Ryan, *This Year I Will...: How to Finally Change a Habit...*
- Mark F. Weinstein, *Habitually Great: Master Your Habits*
- Jack Hodge, *The Power of Habit: Harnessing the Power to Establish Routines that Guarantee Success in Business and Life*
- Debbie Macomber, *Changing Habits*

Self-discipline (self-help books):
- Brian Tracy, *No Excuses!: The Power of Self-Discipline*
- Dalai Lama, *Becoming Enlightened*
- Jim Randel, *The Skinny on Willpower: How to Develop Self-Discipline*
- Eckhart Tolle, *A New Earth: Awakening to Your Life's Purpose*
- Norman Vincent Peale, *The Power of Positive Thinking*

Leadership derailment:
- Sydney Finkelstein, *Why Smart Executives Fail: And What You Can Learn from Their Mistakes*
- Tim Irwin, *Derailed*
- Adrian Turnham, *The Elephant in the Boardroom*

Leadership development:
- Ellen Van Velsor, Cynthia D. McCauley, and Marian N. Ruderman (eds.), *The Center for Creative Leadership Handbook of Leadership Development*
- Morgan McCall, Michael M. Lombardo, and Ann M. Morrison, *Lessons of Experience: How Successful Executives Develop on the Job*
- Morgan McCall, *High Flyers: Developing the Next Generation of Leaders*

Organization execution:
- Ram Charan and Larry Bossidy, *Execution*
- Chris McChesney, Sean Covey, and Jim Huling, *The Four Disciplines of Execution*

From these various yet related literatures, we have culled seven disciplines that instill leadership sustainability:

- Simplicity
- Time
- Accountability
- Resources
- Tracking
- Melioration
- Emotion

These are the next phase of our leadership journey.

These seven disciplines spell the mnemonic *START ME*. We think this is apt because for each of us, sustainability *starts* with *me*. These seven disciplines turn hope into reality. Leaders who apply these disciplines go beyond the *why* and *what* of leadership to reach the *how*. Of course, if leaders lack a strong sense of *why* they should change and *what* they should change to, leadership sustainability does not matter. But once leaders accept the *why* of change and understand the *what,* dealing with *how* will make sure that leadership change happens. These seven disciplines bring order to action planning.

To get a sense of where you stand now with regard to these seven disciplines, read through Exercise 1.1 and jot down a rating from 1 to 5 for each element. A score key follows the exercise.

iphone: **RedLaser**
Android: **Barcode Scanner**

Scan this QR code to find out how sustainable your leadership is with a quick assessment.

leadershipsustainability.com/qr/
preassessment

Exercise 1.1   Summary of the Factors of Leadership Sustainability

Leadership	Key Insight	Diagnostic Question	Rating
Sustainable disciplines	Leadership sustainability increases when leaders...	In my recent efforts to improve as a leader, to what extent did I... or	Low–high 1–5
		In our efforts to improve leadership, to what extent do we ... (note change from "I" to "we" to shift a focus from personal to organizational sustainability)	
Simplicity	Focus on a few key behaviors that have high impact.	Prioritize what I should improve and focus only on a few key behaviors that I could improve?	
Time	Put their desired behaviors into their calendar and monitor how well these behaviors show up in their time allocations.	Translate my desired improvements into specific actions that showed up on my calendar and actually received my time and attention?	

Exercise 1.1   *Summary of the Factors of Leadership Sustainability*
(Continued)

Leadership	Key Insight	Diagnostic Question	Rating
Accountability	Are personally and publicly accountable for making change happen.	Take personal responsibility for making the change happen by publicly declaring my intentions?	
Resources	Support their desired changes with coaching and infrastructure.	Find support to make my desired changes happen?	
Tracking	Measure their behaviors and results in specific ways.	Create indicators to measure and track my progress on making the desired change happen?	
Melioration	Constantly improve by learning from mistakes and failures and demonstrating resilience.	Reflect on what did or did not work and learn from both failures and successes?	
Emotion	Have a personal passion and emotion for the changes they need to make.	Feel passionate about making the desired change because it was something I believed in and was consistent with my values?	

Score key:

1. Compute your total score:
   - 31 to 35: You are a sustainable leader; this book should reinforce what you do.
   - 26 to 30: You are close, but sometimes things don't happen that you think should.
   - 21 to 25: You have quite a bit of success as a leader, but you are not progressing as fast as you would like.
   - Under 20: You like to start things, but you get frustrated that they don't seem to happen as often as you would like.

2. Review individual items. Look at the items where you scored lower (1, 2, or 3), and pay more attention to the chapters that address those disciplines. Often leaders have patterns that limit their ability to sustain change.

Conclusion: Leaders in Flight

We are sure that we have not captured everything that will increase leadership sustainability, but these seven disciplines inform both personal efforts to be a better leader and organizational investments to build better leadership. When leaders make commitments to change something in training, coaching, or performance management, the impact increases when participants attend to these seven disciplines as they anticipate how to turn learning into action. When an aspiring leader receives 360-degree feedback, the personal action plan will be more sustainable when it embodies these insights. When an organization's leadership development plan is reviewed, executives increase confidence that leadership investments will have payback when they rigorously apply the seven disciplines.

Leaders matter. Leadership matters more. Leadership sustainability matters most. Do not walk home.

iphone: **RedLaser**
Android: **Barcode Scanner**

Scan this QR code to download the STARTME app.

leadershipsustainability.com/
qr/app

CHAPTER 2

SIMPLICITY

2

Simplicity is the ultimate sophistication.

—*Leonardo da Vinci*

We live in a complex world that is growing increasingly more complex. We are exposed to 24-hour news cycles that have to be filled. Technology pushes ahead obsessively. The global economy confounds even experts. Politicians caught in the details of defending their positions focus more on reelection than on problem solving. We set goals in January that seem irrelevant in June. We are filled with mild anxiety about what lies ahead. The world is a complex place.

Real-World Complexity

Here are two executives who are cutting through complexity and building simplicity in major organizations.

Bruce Broussard, President, Humana

Humana, Inc., headquartered in Louisville, Kentucky, is a Fortune 100 health-care company. It offers a wide range of insurance products and health and wellness services incorporating an integrated approach to lifelong well-being.

Bruce Broussard previously worked in senior leadership positions at McKesson Specialty Health, US Oncology, US Physical Therapy, HarborDental Properties, and Regency Health Services. This experience in provider health care was critical in his being named president of Humana in November 2011, with the expectation of his becoming CEO on retirement of current CEO, Mike McCallister.

When Broussard came to Humana, he realized that he needed to focus the company on the critical priorities that would help it to succeed in the future. He feels that finding simplicity is one of the hardest things that effective leaders need to do. He looks to successful companies such as Southwest and Apple, where, in the midst of compelling and competing priorities, leaders maintain a simple focus on what's most important.

Without that focus, managers are too often rewarded for lots of activity rather than for making sure that the activity is focused on the right things—they rush about, busy as an ant in an anthill, Broussard says, while the mountain of things that need to be done stays put. Successful organizations keep messages and themes simple, tied to their core value proposition. They stick with these core messages and constantly trim their agenda to the big items without being lured astray by small activities.

At Humana, the board and senior leadership team constantly ask the question, "Is this core activity or investment core to what we are about? Will this move the mountain?" Broussard discovered that Humana's root purpose was to reduce health-care costs and improve the health experiences of its members.

To get to these root purposes, leaders need to ask a lot of questions. In particular, they need to go to key customers and question them to discover their core priorities. Through questions, Broussard was able to identify the simple priorities on which Humana should focus. For example, if Humana customers experience rising health-care costs, the key questions would be

- What is causing the increased health-care costs?
- What decisions lead to increased costs?
- How do leaders make decisions to modify these costs?
- How can members reduce health-care costs by preventive action?
- What can the company do to increase preventive action and enhance members' well-being?

Through simplicity, the company can focus its attention and maintain that focus in the face of increasing complexity.

Thomas Kurian, Executive Vice President of Oracle Product Development

As executive vice president of product development at Oracle, Inc., Thomas Kurian reports to CEO Larry Ellison. He is responsible for leading all aspects of product strategy and software development and delivery of Oracle's software product portfolio, including Oracle Database, Oracle Fusion Middleware, enterprise resource planning (ERP), customer relationship management (CRM), and supply-chain management applications. This software group has 25,000 engineers and ships 3,600 products per year. It is a highly complex organization with a very complicated workload.

Kurian simplifies this complex work into doable tasks by taking three actions:

- He sets clear priorities to remove ambiguity about what's important.
- He targets a few big bets about the future and then builds toward them. The success of these major initiatives must be big; otherwise, they will not take advantage of the opportunity or create enough emotional excitement to sustain themselves.
- He builds a virtuous cycle around the seven disciplines in this book: simplicity, time, accountability, resources, tracking, melioration, and emotion.

Kurian runs a priority-setting exercise with his top team every two years. This exercise creates unity by establishing where the organization is headed and determining how to allocate resources toward its real priorities. This avoids any sense of flavor of the month or confusion about what's important. Currently, Oracle's Product Development Department has three priorities:

Building engineered systems. Kurian's goal in engineered systems is to improve the relationship between software and hardware by at least 10 times and up to 50 times using technology that's currently available.

Aligning to the cloud. Current information systems are inherently complex and on older platforms which slows down the rate at which innovation can happen. By employing cloud technology, innovation is accelerated because people do not have to deal with the bottlenecks associated with getting set up and configured on different platforms.

Making software more accessible. Oracle is building a brand-new suite of packaged solutions that are more accessible for its clients in enterprise, human resources (HR), CRM, and other types of software.

Oracle can't wait to build products when the industry demands them—that would be too slow. Offerings have to be thought out and constructed far in advance so as to be ready for the market. Product Development must have straightforward priorities because the company has too much at risk to thrash around.

Kurian has had real success by starting with simplicity—his priorities and resource allocation to them—and then aligning the other disciplines to get things done. His organization generates new products worth $35 billion every year to keep Oracle growing at its target of 10 percent annually. This is the equivalent of building a huge new software company every year.

Building Simplicity

Like these executives, we all recognize complexity in our everyday lives. We used to have three TV channels, and we complained about phone calls. Now we have hundreds of channels, and the phone seems like the least of our interruptions. We get too much e-mail, and we do not have enough time for all the people who text us or who want to connect through LinkedIn or who want to befriend us on Facebook. We used to worry about local issues in our community or country; now economic patterns force us to be concerned about the entire world. We once trusted big companies, but when Arthur Andersen and then Lehman Brothers collapsed, we realized that even large companies can falter. Now we worry about country collapses as well as company failures. Iceland has already succumbed, and it seems all too likely that Greece and other European Union countries such as Portugal, Spain, and Italy may follow. We grew up with typewriters and letters and then switched to word processors and e-mail, and now it's Facebook, Google, blogs, Short Message Service (SMS) messages, and tweets. What's next?

No one can stay totally informed, connected, or adaptable. When we are overwhelmed with complexity or when we don't understand what's going on, we are not likely to sustain our actions. Karl Weick, a brilliant organization theorist from the University of Michigan, writes, "Chaotic action is better than orderly inaction." This statement implies two levels of action: orderly inaction and chaotic action. In the former, we wait until someone more senior tells us what to do. In the latter, we run around taking action, hoping that we might do something worthwhile. But there is a third level of action to respond to complexity: action based on making informed strategic assumptions about the future.

When leaders such as Broussard and Kurian focus on priorities and take personal responsibility for their actions by making strategic assumptions explicit, they reduce the number of options and shift attention from what could be done to what has most impact. They drive simplicity by using strategic assumptions to answer the question: What is the most important thing we can be working on right now? Leaders sustain desired changes by ensuring simplicity in the face of complexity through focusing on a few targeted personal behaviors they can improve and on the critical few work areas that make the biggest difference. Simplicity leads to sustainability—because without it we chase complexity and never catch up.

Leaders sustain change when they enact the discipline of simplicity in the face of complexity by making strategic assumptions about the future that allow them to take the best course of action today. You can simplify the path forward for yourself and for your organization through three principles of simplicity:

- Focus on what matters most.
- Tell stories.
- Avoid concept clutter.

Focus on What Matters Most

When you have too much to do, don't try to do it all. It is important to learn how to focus on a few critical ideas. With 10 priorities, 100 units of time, energy, and resources divided equally (10 units to each priority) will be too little to get any of them done. To help leaders sustain their goals, we propose three ways to bring strategic assumptions to life by focusing on what matters most:

- Define the problem.
- Prioritize.
- Filter and frame.

Define the Problem

Early in the astronaut program, people say, the National Aeronautics and Space Administration (NASA) discovered that ballpoint pens do not work in zero gravity. To combat the problem, NASA scientists spent years and millions of dollars to develop a pen that writes in zero gravity, upside down, underwater, on almost any surface including glass, and at temperatures ranging from below freezing to 300°C. The Russians used a pencil.

Although apocryphal, this story illustrates how a poor definition of a problem can lead to a series of complex and expensive actions. "Invent a pen to write in zero gravity" turned out to be far costlier than "find something that writes in the conditions of space."

Simplicity arrives when we take the time to accurately define the problems we face. We get caught up in our own version of inventing a pen to write in space because we want to take action. It's seductive to quickly state a problem and then start working on the solution, but as the solution gets complex, we pour on more and more time, money, and resources. It is impossible to keep things simple without a clear definition of the problem to be solved.

As chief information officer (CIO) of a large Chicago-based software company, Ashley wanted to help her employees improve. Omar, one of her direct reports, worked in information technology (IT) for the president of the company's Canadian region. Ashley received strong feedback from the Canadian president that Omar was not "strategic" enough. Ashley had always considered herself to be very strategic and felt that she could help Omar. Her plan:

- Talk to Omar about the feedback.
- Ask him to read articles on what it means to be strategic.
- Fly him to Chicago for a week at corporate headquarters. While there, he would meet several of the senior corporate executives face-to-face, including the boss of the Canadian president.

○ Attend several key meetings so that he could watch Ashley interact with corporate and business people and then debrief each encounter for its strategic significance.

○ Review with Ashley how the corporate IT strategic plan fit with the corporate business plan and with each of the geographies.

○ Develop an action plan for how to be more strategic in his Canadian work.

At the end of the week, Omar returned to Toronto ready to put his action plan to work. Twice a month for six months, Ashley and Omar reviewed progress on the phone. During a midyear leadership conference, Ashley spotted the Canadian president at a break and asked him if he had noticed any improvement in Omar's strategic acumen. The president responded that he had not noticed any improvement. In fact, in his opinion, Omar had gotten worse. When Ashley described what steps she had taken to help Omar, the president responded: "No, no. When I said he was not strategic I meant that he talked too much in meetings and didn't listen to what others on the management team need him to do. He has an IT agenda, not a business agenda. Since he has come back from Chicago, he is even more adamant about telling us what we need based on his meetings with our corporate executives. What he needs to do is shut up and listen before he tells us what IT will do."

Ashley was astounded. She had not listened carefully to this executive, and in her haste to help Omar's performance, she had solved the wrong problem and made things worse for both of them.

At our company, The RBL Group, we often teach others how to be more effective coaches. Virtually every coaching engagement begins with defining the problem before solving it. Taking the time to define the problem stumps many leaders. It's easily the toughest part of coaching to teach. Coaches and leaders often work to fix symptoms, not underlying problems. The symptom is the presenting challenge, the problem is why this symptom exists and persists. Leaders need to probe "why" the challenge exists until they find a root cause. We coach coaches to ask up to five "why's" to define the underlying problem that needs to be addressed. And even if someone does recognize the importance of problem solving in a workshop setting, it's apt to be the first thing he or she forgets to do when he or she returns to work. Like Ashley, managers love to hear a quick version of the symptoms and promptly offer ideas on how to solve it. This almost always frustrates the person being coached because the coach doesn't understand enough to be helpful, and fixing symptoms is almost always short term.

Prioritize

Scott is the new CEO of a Colorado tech company that—after struggling for several years—had just tried to merge with a larger company and failed. Prior to his new role, Scott had spent several years as a successful executive at Xerox. His biggest surprise in his new role was the culture of entitlement that the tech company had developed. He referred to it as a "lifestyle company"—a place where people frequently took time off to ski when a snowstorm hit the area or to hit the trails with a mountain bike or a good pair of boots on any nice day during the year.

Scott knew that he had to get his top leaders to prioritize and change their behaviors if they were ever going to turn the company around. He managed to cut the pressure a bit by reducing costs through some product and process changes that achieved modest success. However, he knew that the real problem was the culture. Employees and key leaders acted as though the company's success was not as important as their lifestyle. He felt that he was the only one who had a different agenda.

After much contemplation, he decided to engage his top 100 leaders in a global leadership conference held at a hotel near corporate headquarters, and he asked RBL Group to act as facilitator. On the first day, Scott confessed how frustrated he was with the current situation and asked his leaders to use the conference as a way to identify cultural priorities to change their own behavior. On the first day, people sat at breakout tables and shared their hopes and fears about the company and what they would do to change their behavior in ways more congruent with a performance culture. These responses were summarized and handed out to each person. This list of brainstormed responses was boiled down to the top three behaviors that each leader should do to successfully implement the new culture.

On the second day, Scott used the RBL "Culture Virus Detector" exercise with the group. Given the conversation from the first day about new leadership behaviors, we asked the 10 breakout tables to identify the most malevolent cultural virus from a list of about 40 possibilities. Some examples:

- *Overinform.* Tell everybody, and then have a meeting. We make sure that everyone has been touched before we meet, which slows down our ability to reach decisions.
- *Have it my way.* We don't learn much from each other—the "not invented here syndrome."
- *Saturday morning team captain.* We enjoy criticizing everything, even before it happens.
- *False positive.* We feign agreement, we hide the ultimate conclusions, and we think the goal will please everyone. This leads to passive resistance.
- *Hard on the people instead of the problem.* We attack a colleague personally rather than attacking the problem; we find scapegoats.

We expected the 10 tables to pick 8 or 10 different viruses. But that did not happen. Of the 10 tables, 6 independently settled on one virus:

- *Flavor of the month.* We jump from program to program as separate, not integrated initiatives, and cynicism about new programs mounts.

The other four tables also shared a choice:

- *Disjointed action.* We don't see the big picture and how our unit's work relates to the group or fits in with an overall strategy.

Scott had landed on a way to talk about cultural priorities in a manner that allowed his team to start setting them. Sensing that this was an important breakthrough, Scott asked each table to draw a picture on a flipchart of how the chosen virus manifested in the company. The drawings were not beautiful or artistic, but they captured the essence of their behavior and the problems they caused. We spent the rest of the day developing action plans for how to resolve the two cultural virus priorities. Each team presented their improvement ideas to the entire group, and then each leader signed his or her flipchart picture as a token of his or her commitment to resolve the virus.

It was clear that these cultural issues were deeply embedded, so Scott proposed a novel solution to keep the issues a top priority. Each of the 10 pictures was saved and framed. The 10 crudely drawn flipchart pages then were displayed in the front hall of the corporate office where everyone would be reminded when they came to work or visited corporate headquarters. Scott wanted these pictures to stay on their minds as real priorities to resolve. He wanted everyone to be focused and feel an urgency to get those pictures removed. They all agreed that the only way they would take down the pictures was through a unanimous agreement at their next leadership conference that was scheduled the following year.

The strange pictures hanging on the wall at corporate headquarters were an ongoing reminder that leaders needed to resolve the problems they represented. Leaders challenged one another when they saw dysfunctional behavior—such as hitting the slopes after a snowstorm when there were unresolved client priorities. Engineers worked late when they had to. Over time, a palpable change emerged, and people started getting into the technical challenges of the business and solving client problems. The culture was evolving.

The following year, there was unanimous agreement that they had resolved the flavor-of-the-month virus. However, the disjointed-action virus was still not fully resolved. So 6 of the 10 pictures were ceremoniously taken down from the hallway and brought to the center of the room and placed in a large fireproof container, where a man in a fireproof suit used a blowtorch on them. The 100 leaders in the room cheered as the virus pictures burned. Their success in changing their behavior and their culture was represented symbolically in the pictures burning in the container. The next year the remaining four pictures also were burned. More important, Scott had led his leaders in a prioritization process that resulted in significant improvements in their behavior and in their culture. By focusing on specific problems represented by the virus pictures, leaders had significantly adjusted the culture in a positive way.

Setting priorities separates the urgent from the important, focuses on actions with high impact and ease of implementation, and emphasizes lead not lag actions. Yet, at the heart of setting priorities is the art of learning to say no to some things and yes to a critical few others. In a world of complexity, leaders have too many things they can change. In the spirit of strategic assumptions and Betty Ford, just say no. You don't have to do everything. Instead, the best leaders do a few things really well. Scott's focus on identifying and then resolving two cultural viruses is an excellent example of focusing on the few that you will do well and saying no to the rest. By saying no to lower priorities, leaders say yes to the things that are most important and get on the right track toward sustaining relevant changes.

Filter and Frame

We attend many company leadership conferences every year. Before speaking, we've found, it is always a good idea to get a sense of the group by arriving early to observe and learn from the interaction. The intent of doing this is to filter what's important in the dialogue and to build it into our talks. At one large conference last year, the head of strategy gave a 90-minute presentation with the title, "Clarifying Our Strategic Position." His PowerPoint deck contained 47 slides with 11-point font size, and each slide crammed with statistics, and financial and operational terms. It was interesting to watch the participants in the room, who occupied their 90 minutes by texting and e-mailing or doodling on their papers. It was fun (though perhaps rude) to stand up as the next speaker and ask, "So what's your strategy?" and watch everyone flounder. No one could respond clearly.

The point here is not that the information was irrelevant or that the head of strategy did not know his material. Rather, he presented too much detail without picking out the key points of the data and rallying the group for action, so he lost his opportunity to have sustainable impact as a leader. Too much information is boring because it doesn't serve as a guide to focus action on what is most important.

When presenting complex information, it's essential to filter the data, identify the critical two or three important ideas, and organize data into patterns—then frame a go-forward set of actions that are congruent.

In the case of the head of strategy, the information—when he finally filtered it—was not boring at all. He opened his next presentation with the filtered and focused conclusions: "Our costs are too high, and our productivity is below industry standards. I have detail that backs this up, but there is no doubt that we need to find ways to drive these costs down." At the end of his presentation, he reiterated his conclusions and then did a call for action to change. As the saying goes, to sustain an idea, tell people what you are going to tell them (by filtering out what is most important to tell), tell them (the key issues), and then tell them what you told them (repeat the key issues). And the head of strategy then went beyond this old formula by asking several in the audience for their ideas about what they should do to change.

When you assemble a big jigsaw puzzle, it's natural to start with the edges because they provide a framework in which the other pieces fit. They simplify a complex activity and allow the picture to take shape. Likewise, when leaders can frame their complex problems by defining boundaries, they are more able to sustain their desired changes. Leaders who see patterns in data constantly look for common themes, messages, or implications. They often draw configurations that capture the patterns. They look for the simple messages.

When Starbucks grew rapidly in the 1990s, many employees were overwhelmed by the growth pressures. Leaders instituted institutional habits for baristas called the *LATTE method:* listen, acknowledge, take action, thank the customer, and explain why the problem occurred. This simple framework allowed Starbuck's employees to sustain their growth agenda.[1]

Framing is a skill that leads to and demands focus because it demands the ability to synthesize. The process of effective framing can be seen as a diamond, as shown in Figure 2.1.

Figure 2.1   *The process of framing ideas to focus attention.*

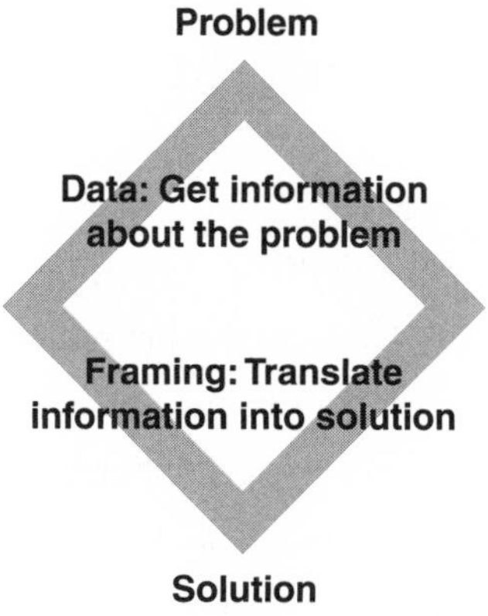

Problem

Data: Get information about the problem

Framing: Translate information into solution

Solution

At the top of the diamond is the initial presenting challenge, which has no preconceived solutions. To solve the problem, it's necessary to collect data about possible ways to resolve the problem. It's not uncommon for people to think that they have solved the problem when they have data about it. This was the case with the head of strategic planning who presented the boring presentation. He knew a lot about the industry and about his company's operational and financial conditions, but he didn't have a way to make sense of the information for people. It's not until the problem is framed that there can be a point of view about what to do with the data. The diamond shape represents these steps well. The problem represents the intent for a solution. The diamond shape widens out to represent data gathering and then narrows once the data have been framed toward a solution.

To focus and drive sustainable action, a leader must frame the information. This allows complex data to be understood as part of a pattern.

One key to effective framing is to find common patterns to organize diverse ideas. For example, a leader attends a training program and learns lots of concepts, frameworks, ideas, and tools. These options can be transferred from ideas to practice by finding the patterns in the complex ideas. We like to look for underlying concepts that simplify complex ideas. To create a typology, ask: What do these concepts have in common? How do they differ? What are some common underlying dimensions that can be used to organize the ideas?

Jordan, head of operations for a beverage company, realized that over the past six months his organization had adopted more than 100 initiatives it planned to implement over the next three years. Jordan was convinced that this 100-initiative list not only was confusing but also was certain to result in significant overload for the employees. So he pulled together a team of high-potential leaders and spent a morning looking for ways to consolidate activities. After a few hours, they winnowed the list down to 40 initiatives.

Jordan believed that this was still too complex to sustain action. As he worked with his team, members organized the 40 separate initiatives into common clusters of ideas, some focused on the future and some on the present, some focused outside and some inside. With these dimensions, they could then talk about four focus areas and specific initiatives within each area. This framing effort produced a chart that showed the 40 initiatives in easily grasped sets and vastly simplified Jordan's task of communicating what would be happening over the next few years and when. Table 2.1 is an extract from the chart showing eight samples of surviving initiatives.

You already have a lot of experience with framing. Just think of a restaurant menu. If you took the items individually, you might have 70 or 80 choices, but restaurants cluster their offerings into drinks, appetizers, salads, main courses, desserts, and after-dinner drinks. These categories make ordering simpler. Years ago, when buying a car, a buyer was forced to consider dozens of independent options. Today, these many options are clustered into package A, package B, or package C. This simplifies the decision while still giving the car buyer a sense of personal choice. Similar package deals are offered in fast food restaurants, weekend lodging getaways, computer software, and home cable television. Leaders who bundle complex issues into simple solutions likely sustain their actions.

Table 2.1   Framing Initiatives into Clusters

Time Horizon		
Locus of Impact	Present (Impact in the Next 12 Months)	Future (Impact in 12 to 36 Months)
Internal	Initiatives that impact employees in the next year: • Restructure shared services. • Revise incentive program for sales.	Initiatives that impact employees after this year: • Revise executive compensation approach. • Measure impact of leadership development program.
External	Initiatives that impact customers, vendors, or the community in the next year: • Focus on core beverage advertising. • Measure "share of stomach" in key EU markets.	Initiatives that impact customers, vendors, or the community more than a year out: • Brand health benefits of core beverage in Southeast Asian markets. • Initiate global vendor-of-choice program to reduce costs.

Tell Stories, Create a Narrative

Good strategy tells a story that trumps data. Sustainable strategy creates a narrative and puts an individual story into context. If two people present to a group with the intent of persuading the group to do something and one uses data and the other tells a simple, relevant story, the storyteller is almost always more persuasive. People grow up teaching and learning through stories. Stories filter a lot of data because they embed strategic assumptions. They do this because the story conveys what is most important to pay attention to and what happens if the priorities are not considered. Stories make change personal because at their core they teach lessons about people. Stories also do a lot to create a personal desire for change and improvement because they describe a gap between where we are today and where we desire to be in the future. So leaders can sustain change by telling personal stories about who they and their people could be if they sustain the change. As separate stories weave around common themes, they create a sustainable narrative.

Tell Stories that Create a Narrative Focused on the Future

There are two ways a leader can create a need for change. One is to refer to a "burning platform"—a metaphor suggesting that we are standing on a surface that is on fire, and therefore, to save our lives, we all must get moving right now. This leader creates action by pointing to major customer complaints, product flaws, competitive threats, or other bad things that will cause failure if people don't do something about them.

The other approach is for the leader to tell a story that describes the gap between how things are today and how we'd like them to be in the future. Martin Luther King did a brilliant job of creating a narrative about a world without racism in his "I have a dream" speech:

> I have a dream that one day this nation will rise up and live out the true meaning of its creed: "We hold these truths to be self-evident: that all men are created equal."
>
> I have a dream that one day on the red hills of Georgia the sons of former slaves and the sons of former slave owners will be able to sit down together at the table of brotherhood.
>
> I have a dream that one day even the state of Mississippi, a state sweltering with the heat of injustice, sweltering with the heat of oppression, will be transformed into an oasis of freedom and justice.
>
> I have a dream that my four little children will one day live in a nation where they will not be judged by the color of their skin but by the content of their character.
>
> I have a dream today.

What makes this story so powerful is that King outlines the future and then goes back and forth between the future and the present day to illustrate the gap:

> I have a dream that one day, down in Alabama, with its vicious racists, with its governor having his lips dripping with the words of interposition and nullification; one day right there in Alabama, little black boys and black girls will be able to join hands with little white boys and white girls as sisters and brothers.
>
> I have a dream today.

A powerful narrative creates a need for change by showing the gap between the possible futures if we take action now contrasted with the likely outcomes of the status quo. Future-oriented stories are powerful because they are concrete examples of what could be.

Tell Stories that Build a Narrative and Line of Sight Among Ideas

Some companies use an avatar to build a line of sight between their employees and their target customer. Apple sponsored a series of comical commercials featuring "Microsoft Man" and "Apple Boy" that demonstrated the very different philosophies of the two companies. Gap's Old Navy Division uses "Jenny"—one of the most popular names for women born in 1979—for a composite designed to represent the 29-year-old mother who is the sweet spot of the chain's target customers (who are between 25 and 35).

A few years ago, Old Navy lost sales after it alienated its target customers by abandoning basic merchandise such as Capri pants and T-shirts featuring its logos and switching much of its focus to younger customers and products fashionable among that group. "We've gone to a massive disconnect" with our target shopper, said Tom Wyatt, president of Gap (MarketWatch, October 16, 2008). "Now we have a clear understanding of who we serve. Basics are important to Jenny."

He added, "We are not H&M" (referring to the low-budget Swedish fashion retailer).

On a visit to Gap headquarters in San Francisco, we were struck by the prevalence of Jenny. Life-sized cutouts of Jenny in action—making decisions about what clothes to buy her family—are everywhere. When a new line is successful, Jenny explains the success to employees. When a new line is not successful, Jenny explains what she didn't like.

The use of Jenny allows Gap leaders to build a line of sight across complicated issues faced by their target shopper—the economy, children in school, and so on—and from their customers to their employees. It's difficult to help someone in the abstract. Employees get to know Jenny because they have made her real. Because Jenny seems like a real person, with real needs, it's easier to help her and know what to suggest for her and her family.

Tell Stories that Make Heroes of People Who Support Your Agenda

Another way that leaders can get people on the same page to ensure a simple, common agenda that is sustainable is to tell stories that make heroes out of your people who take action consistent with what you want to be known for. Recently, we read a blog post where Christopher Elliot relates a story that Southwest Airlines tells about one of its pilots:

> Last night, my husband and I got the tragic news that our three-year-old grandson in Denver had been murdered by our daughter's live-in boyfriend.
>
> He is being taken off life support tonight at nine o'clock, and his parents have opted for organ donation, which will take place immediately. Over 25 people will receive his gift tonight, and many lives will be saved.

This morning, after only a couple hours' sleep, my husband and I began to make arrangements to get to Denver to be with our daughter. He is currently on business in LA and is flying Southwest.

While his employer, Northrop Grumman, made arrangements to get his ticket changed so he could get to Tucson today (which he had to do in order to not spend any extra money), I called Southwest to arrange his flight from Tucson to Denver so he would be stepping off one plane and getting on another. I'm actually her stepmother and it's much more important for my husband to be there than for me to be there.

In LAX, the lines to both check a bag and get through security were exceptional. He got to the airport two hours early and was still late getting to his plane.

Every step of the way, he's on the verge of tears and trying to get assistance from both TSA and Southwest employees to get to his plane on time.

According to him, everyone he talked to couldn't have cared less. When he was done with security, he grabbed his computer bag, shoes, and belt and ran to his gate in his stocking feet.

When he got there, the pilot of his plane and the ticketing agent both said, "Are you Mark? We held the plane for you, and we're so sorry about the loss of your grandson."

The pilot held the plane that was supposed to take off at 11:50 until 12:02 when my husband got there.

As my husband walked down the jetway with the pilot, he said, "I can't thank you enough for this."

The pilot responded with, "They can't go anywhere without me, and I wasn't going anywhere without you. Now relax. We'll get you there. And again, I'm so sorry."

My husband was able to take his first deep breath of the day.

I don't know any other airline that would have done this.

I'm speechless. Twelve minutes may not sound like a lot to you or me, but every second counts when you're an airline. Southwest can turn an entire plane around in about 20 minutes, so 12 minutes is half an eternity.

I shared Nancy's story with Southwest, and a representative said that the airline was "proud" of the way the pilot had held the flight. Again, most airlines would punish an employee who holds up the line for any reason.[2]

This story about the pilot is a central plot for Southwest. This pilot not only held the plane, but he went also outside the plane to greet the customer to let him know how much he cared. Typically, Southwest wants to be known as fun, on time, and cheap—but even more than that, Southwest wants people to know that it cares about its customers.

As these individual hero stories get shared, they create a sustainable narrative about what is expected and valued. As a leader looking for the right hero to tell a story about, first clarify your customer value proposition. What is most important to how you want your customers to view you? Typically, you have five choices. All are important, but if you had to allocate 100 points to the five choices, which one would get 60 points?

- Best quality and performance
- Best service
- Most innovative
- Lowest price
- Fastest

Most Southwest stories are about low prices. However, the pilot helping the customer in need is about the company's service and caring nature. When you are clear about your story, communicate the value proposition to your customers and to your employees. Then start looking for employees who are doing a great job of delivering that value. Make these people your heroes because they are delivering value to your customers the right way. If you do it enough, you will have delivered a simple message that drives others to act in similar ways.

Avoid Concept Clutter

Concept clutter is all around us—and it piles up in heaps around leadership. When you feed the words *leader* and *leadership* into Google, you get 1.2 billion hits. That's concept clutter. Concept clutter builds up about a lot of other things too. Most of your employees face multiple mixed messages about what's important for them to do every day. How do you cut through the muddle to get direct action? Broussard and Kurian at the beginning of the chapter turned concept clutter into priorities. Likewise, in *Steve Jobs*, Walter Isaacson describes Jobs's approach like this:

> Once a year Jobs took his most valuable employees on a retreat, which he called "The Top 100."... Jobs would stand in front of a whiteboard... and ask, "What are the ten things we should be doing next?" People would fight to get their suggestions on the list. Then Jobs would slash the bottom seven and announce, "We can only do three."

Perhaps a primary reason Steve Jobs accomplished as much as he did was his ability to focus and get others to focus with him. He was a master at eliminating concept clutter and getting people focused on what is important. This skill is one that must be honed continually, or people get mired in the complexity of the moment.

Concept clutter is not just a matter of setting too many goals, as the Steve Jobs example indicates. It finds its way into reports and presentations. A year or so ago we attended a conference where someone in the audience yelled "Bingo!" about 10 minutes into a PowerPoint presentation given by one of our consulting staff. Apparently some of the audience had made a buzzword bingo game and handed it out to many in the audience. To the embarrassment of the presenter, his presentation had quickly filled up the bingo sheets.

We find variations of this when we work with new consultants who are preparing reports for clients. It's easy for them to use technical jargon and buzzwords that sound important but make it harder to read the report. When we see this clutter, we read a paragraph together and then ask, "What does this mean?" Usually the consultant is very bright and can answer this question clearly. Then we ask for a rewrite of the paragraph using simpler language to get that kind of clarity on paper. If you think people might yell out "Bingo!" during your presentations or while reading a report you have written, you should give some real thought to simplification. The best ways to simplify are to state the essence of the idea and to cut out the rest.

One tool that stands above others to reduce clutter is the one-page memo, which is one of the cultural fixtures at Procter & Gamble (P&G). After graduate school, Norm went to work at a P&G startup plant in rural Georgia. He soon learned that every internal communication was required to fit on one page and follow a fixed format, and this remains a very powerful discipline for cutting through concept clutter. The startup plant was a very large capital expenditure, but its logic was still contained on a one-page memo. When employees at the plant were learning how to write their own memos, that one was used as the prime example. How many of us would need more than one page to ask for something as complex as the startup capital for a new plant? How thick is the request likely to be? And yet there it was—on one page.

Each one-page memo has five parts:

1. *The idea.* A one-sentence proposal about what is desired.
2. *Background.* What conditions have led you to this recommendation? This is the basis for discussion, so it must be nondebatable facts.
3. *How it works.* The details: What, who, when, where, and how?

4. *Benefits.* The *why* of the idea. There are typically three benefits:
   - The recommended action is tied to the business strategy.
   - It's already proven in a test market or in another business unit.
   - It is profitable.

     The strategy linkage demonstrates that you are doing the right thing. The second and third benefits demonstrate that you are doing things the right way—you're effective (proven to work) and efficient (profitable).
5. *Next steps.* Who has to do what and by when?

P&G understands the importance of keeping things simple. Anyone who has been through it will tell you that it takes more work to write a one-page memo than it does to write a 10-page memo.

A 10-page white paper often obfuscates, whereas a one-page memo simplifies and clarifies. Eliminating clutter is a key discipline for ensuring simplicity by getting to the essence.

If you want to ensure simplicity, we challenge you to pilot one-page memos in your organization. Be the first in your area to introduce the one-page memo to reduce concept clutter. Tell others about your intent to reduce complexity. Find an initiative or a situation that is inherently complex, and describe your approach to your memo in the five steps given earlier. Then get the process started:

- Ask your direct reports and peers to challenge your memo— What's missing? What's good about this approach? What have you lost by using it?
- Start your meetings by asking if anyone has written a one-page memo on the topic.
- Celebrate those who are early adopters of the memo format.
- Give a nonfinancial reward to the best one-page memo of the week, the month, the year.

The process of asking for less clutter and more focus on the priorities directs your behavior and the behavior of others toward sustainability.

Conclusion: Leaders as Taxonomists

The goal of taxonomy is to find simple patterns in complex circumstances. This chapter maintains that leaders get things done when they are able to cut through complexity and make the future clearer and simpler. They make things clearer and simpler by finding the essence of what's important and then focusing on that. They tell stories and create narratives about people who are exemplars, and they cut through concept clutter.

Try the following test to determine your predisposition to complexity or simplicity (on a scale of 1 = low to 10 = high):

1. I spend enough time defining a problem before I try to solve it.
2. When I sponsor a new initiative, I'm good at prioritizing the most important factors.
3. After discussions about a topic, I filter the many ideas and summarize them for my team so that we know what's important and can stay on track.
4. I'm good at framing multiple ideas into a coherent game plan.
5. I tend to take a "small wins" approach and sequence the series of accomplishments into a tipping point rather than trying to pull off complicated grand plans.
6. I'm good at telling stories about how it will be in the future if we are successful.
7. When I tell stories, I am able to build a clear line of sight between where we are now and where we want to be.
8. I tell stories about the heroes of my agenda—people who do the right things the right way.

9. I avoid concept clutter by sticking to the essence of an idea when I do presentations.
10. I avoid buzzwords and technical jargon.

Scoring

- *Less than 40:* You are making things much too complicated—you want action, but you have not defined outcomes. Your team is not clear about what you want from them. Make copies of this chapter and read it once a week.
- *41–60:* You are comfortable with complexity, but others are often unsure of what you really want.
- *61–80:* You tend to keep things simple for others but have occasional lapses where you look behind you for your team and can't find them.
- *81–100:* Your team always knows where you stand. You are clear about what you want and when you want it, and you reward others for doing it.

iphone: **RedLaser**
Android: **Barcode Scanner**

Scan this QR code to determine your predisposition to complexity or simplicity.

leadershipsustainability.com/qr/ simplicityassessment

CHAPTER 3

TIME

3

What you do speaks so loud I cannot hear what you say.

—Ralph Waldo Emerson

For leaders who want to sustain their desires and make change happen, *time* means that the future is not bound by the past and that behavioral cycles can be consciously modified. Time becomes a key discipline for sustainability because leaders who want to demonstrate a new behavior or create a new pattern of behaviors can do so only by being intentional about their use of time. Time is both a fixed asset (we all have the same amount of time) and a variable asset (we conceive of and use our time differently).

Real-World Use of Time

How you spend your time defines you as a leader. Here is how one executive made his own place in the sun.

Majed Romaithi, Executive Director of the Real Estate and Infrastructure Department, Abu Dhabi Investment Authority

The Abu Dhabi Investment Authority (ADIA) is a globally diversified investment institution whose sole mission is to invest funds on behalf of the government of the Emirate of Abu Dhabi so as to secure and maintain the future welfare of the Emirate. It is considered one of the largest sovereign wealth funds in the world, making it one of the world's largest institutional investors.

Majed Romaithi is executive director of ADIA's Real Estate and Infrastructure Department. When we talked with him about timing, his perspective was different from what we typically hear in the West and one that we admire as an important tenet about personal responsibility. He believes that the best leaders are those who make the time to drive change wherever it's needed, even if it doesn't fall directly within their formal domain. This means identifying areas that can be improved and doing what it takes to manage the change successfully.

Romaithi—a gifted storyteller—shared a vivid example of his own personal experience with allocating his time beyond his official area of responsibility. In the late 1990s, while training as an equity analyst and working hard to be successful in this role, he was called to a meeting with ADIA's managing director, HH Sheikh Ahmed Bin Zayed Al Nahyan. The managing director shared his vision of a well-developed cadre of Emirati talent across the organization and asked Romaithi for his views on how best to achieve this. After some discussion, they agreed on two key questions:

- Are we recruiting the right people?
- Do we have an effective talent and leadership development system?

The managing director did not instruct Romaithi to do anything specific. But Romaithi saw what needed to be done; he put these issues on his calendar and began tackling them with passion. Having no formal background in human resources (HR), he attended many training courses and read extensively on the subject. A year later, he met with the managing director and presented some ideas on how to answer the two questions and deliver on his vision. Because Romaithi understood the company's routines and the key trigger points of senior ADIA leaders, he was able to frame his new agenda in a way that had real impact quickly. As a result, he was given the task of implementing these ideas and appointed head of learning and development, reporting directly to the managing director, as well as continuing in a limited leadership role in other financial areas.

By 2003, Romaithi was running HR for ADIA and had begun working closely with the managing director to transform all of ADIA's HR operations and introduce global best practices. After building the HR Department, he moved to head up the Real Estate and Infrastructure Department. Simply stated, he spent almost 13 years resolving a problem no one had asked him to tackle. And his career flourished because of it.

As Romaithi reflects on his career, he says that his work in HR has had a much bigger impact on ADIA than any of the work he has done in investments. His personal passion is to involve himself in issues that make a real difference and get those issues on his calendar to improve the institution for the future. He finishes the story, pauses, and finally says: "There are always very important things in life that we can't find time for. We convince ourselves that they can wait, and with that we miss great opportunities to make a difference."

Romaithi's ability to spend time on both asked and unasked priorities demonstrates good leadership.

The Mirror of Truth

We recently had the privilege of coaching a newly installed CEO. As we talked to him, we started with some very simple questions: "What do you want to accomplish in your tenure? What are your priorities?" Through the ideas and tools suggested in Chapter 2, he was able to simplify and focus his agenda. He became clear about his goal: customer-driven innovation. He wanted to become the best in his industry to anticipate and meet future customer needs.

Then we posed the next sustainability question: How credibly do you use your time to accomplish your focus? To test whether his behavior matched his intent, we looked at his calendar for the preceding year. What percentage of his time had he spent on key customers and innovation? Was he spending time with his target customers to learn from them how they were using his products? Was he spending time with thought leaders both inside and outside his company who had innovative ideas he could adapt?

The calendar analysis revealed that most of his time was invested in operational excellence issues, such as financial monitoring, process-control engineering, and reliability improvements. Over the past year, customer-driven innovation issues had been marginal to how he actually spent his time. His actions did not match his rhetoric. He realized that he had spent his time as chief operating officer (COO) focused on delivering results—and he continued to do so as CEO. From here we worked with him to reprioritize where he should spend his time in the next 3, 6, and 12 months to communicate the importance of customer-driven innovation. With whom should he meet? Where should he meet them? What questions should he be asking?

The study and practice of time have been a fertile ground for philosophers who see time as one of the seven quantities that comprise the universe,[1] for scientists who study the evolution of time,[2] for economists who track the use of time (time is money), and for clerics who prophesize the consequences of how time is used. In all these and many other cases, time becomes both a linear concept (we have yesterdays, todays, and tomorrows) and a circular concept (days, seasons, and other patterns govern our lives).

Leadership hypocrisy exists when espoused aspirations are not reflected in actions. The CEO who talked about customer-driven innovation but spent his time doing operational excellence would not like to be called a hypocrite, but in fact he was. Ultimately, leaders speak with their actions more than with their words, with their hands more than with their voices, and with their feet more than with their rhetoric. Leaders with great aspirations but negligible actions create cynicism and turn hope into despair.

In our coaching we often remind leaders of the common human tendency to judge ourselves by our intentions and others by their behaviors. A leader who intends to innovate but does not spend time listening to lighthouse customers, seeking out thought leaders, encouraging dissent, sponsoring new projects, or asking probing questions will not be credible as an innovator, and innovation will not be sustained.

Leaders always have a mirror in which to view themselves, a mirror that will replace hypocrisy with credibility: the calendar. A calendar reflects what we do and not what we say, and it offers an honest look at our priorities, both past and future. Distorting or ignoring the evidence of this mirror inevitably leads to unrealistic expectations and false hopes.

Mastery of Time

How we invest and spend our time defines who we are, what we believe, and who matters most to us. Malcolm Gladwell proposed that a key to outstanding success in any given field is 10,000 hours of experience and practice. The typical Olympic hopeful will train for about four hours a day for at least 310 days a year for six years before making the national team. Likewise, a leader who really means to get outstanding results must invest time on the things that matter most and not be sidetracked by peripherals. For Romaithi, the focus on people became critical to both his and the company's long-term success.

We suggest seven principles on how sustainable leaders consciously master time:

- Take a regular calendar test.
- See yourself as others see you.
- Recognize routines.
- See triggers.
- Start small, and build to a tipping point.
- Manage signals and symbols.
- Be consistent.

Take a Regular Calendar Test

To develop awareness of how you spend your time, begin by articulating your priorities—set out what you see as most important to success in your role. Then look back through your calendar to see how much time you spent on those priorities. This is often done with the following steps:

Step 1: Define success. I will be effective as a leader when I....
Step 2: Audit the calendar. In the last 90 days, how much time did I devote to the desired behaviors?
Step 3: Turn intent into action. What behaviors will I see more of and less of as I accomplish my definition of success?

Henry Mintzberg popularized the research on leader calendar tests in his classic study on the nature of managerial work.[3] Using time logs, he was able to show the fragmentation of managerial behavior with a preference for action, verbal and informal media, and contacts outside the organization. Based on these actions, he identified 10 managerial working roles (interpersonal roles—figurehead, leader, liaison; informational roles—monitor, disseminator, spokesperson; and decisional roles—entrepreneur, disturbance handler, resource allocator, and negotiator).

We adapted this methodology to a study in a large global organization. The headquarters leaders knew the importance of local leaders who both implemented corporate directions and adapted to local conditions. As a first step, we identified over 100 directives from the headquarters about how local leaders should spend their time. We then asked local leaders how much time it would take for them to fulfill the corporate directives. Their answer was about 90 hours a week. We then had local leaders keep a time log of their work for a two-week period, noting every 15 minutes what they were doing. We found that local leaders were working about 45 hours a week. But when we compared what they were actually doing with what they were directed to do by corporate headquarters, the overlap was only about 40 percent. That is, 60 percent of their time was spent responding to local demands with activities unforeseen or unappreciated by corporate leaders. This information enabled a robust discussion that resulted in the corporate leaders significantly simplifying their expectations, focusing on principles more than specific actions. Corporate leaders also streamlined the few priorities that were essential to the overall corporate agenda and then gave discretion to the local leaders to do the right things for their constituents.

We have also used calendar tests in coaching individual leaders. The calendar test can look back to see how leaders used time and look forward to preview how leaders should use their time. Sometimes these calendar-based coaching sessions focus on work-related activities. In the case at the beginning of this chapter, the new CEO improved his focus on customer-driven innovation by consciously managing his calendar and by focusing his return on time invested (ROTI). To encourage customer innovation, he addressed the following questions:

- *With whom do I meet?* He spent significant time inside his company with research and development (R&D) and advanced marketing staff, making himself the head of the innovation committee. He also spent time with lighthouse customers who were experimenters of new ideas and thought leaders in academia and other settings who were probing new ideas related to their areas of interest.

- *Where do I meet?* He consciously chose to visit innovators in their offices and work settings so that he could see and experience how they approached work. This allowed him to send a symbolic message that innovation was so important to him that he would go out of his office to find it.

- *What do we talk about?* He made a deliberate effort to include innovation case studies and statistics in his public appearances and private conversations. He made customer innovation the first item on the corporate executive committee agenda.

His calendar began to match his intentions, and he was able to shift his identity from a COO focused on efficiency to a CEO dedicated to innovation.

Sometimes calendar-based coaching helps leaders to balance work/life tradeoffs. Some CEOs *say* that they value personal and family time, but their actions do not reflect it. We have encouraged leaders we coach who espouse family values to actually apply those values by including time with family on their calendars.

Taking a calendar test does not require a coach. By being conscious of how well professional and personal priorities match with time, any leader can self-monitor and make sure that use of time really reflects priorities. Many people take an annual physical to check if they are healthy and fit. We advocate that leaders do an annual calendar check to see if their public and strategic intentions are consistent with their private and daily actions. Employees, customers, investors, and other stakeholders will be more influenced by behavior than by rhetoric. (Exercise 3.1 provides a worksheet for calendar tests.)

Exercise 3.1   Doing a Calendar Test

Step	Question	Application
1. Define success	I will be effective as a leader when I ...	
2. Audit your calendar	In the last 90 days, how much of my behavior reflects the definition of success in step 1?	
3. Turn intention into action	What behaviors will I see more of and less of as I accomplish my definition of success?	

See Yourself as Others See You

The calendar test is not merely a personal leader mirror. It is also a way to examine how others may perceive you. When we teach workshops, one of the best predictors of whether we have been successful in our teaching is if we are able to see how the material we are teaching is being received by those we are teaching. Good teaching is not just about presenting what we know; it is about ensuring that what we know influences those being taught—that is, less about the ideas and more about the impact of those ideas. The most profound teaching experiences are those where we can see people processing, adapting, and using our ideas to make changes in their lives even as we teach.

Likewise, leaders who want to sustain change should be both doers and observers of their work. Ron Heifetz and Don Laurie call this "leading from the balcony."[4] Leaders should observe whether others are appropriately receiving their personal intentions. When the CEO described earlier visited targeted customers, he could observe how they responded to him and his visit. Were they forthcoming with real information or regaling him with canned presentations? Were they willing to partner with his company to solve new problems? Did his employees who worked directly with customers have good relationships with them? After his visit, were the customers' ideas woven into his company's actions? Essentially, he could observe the impact of his actions even while he was taking them.

We have coached leaders to "have their head on a swivel" so that they can see the impact of their behaviors. One senior executive consistently asked probing and demanding questions of her staff. When we asked her to reflect on her behavior, she recognized that while her intent was to use difficult questions to evoke deeper insights, her staff mostly gave her superficial answers, hoping to move the conversation along quickly. She was not able to sustain her goals as a leader because she was not fully aware of the impact of her actions on others.

Leadership is accomplished only with and through others. When leaders see how their use of time affects others, they are more able to gain commitment. Leaders can ask the following questions to better understand the impact of their use of time:

- Who are the people I need to connect with to accomplish my goals?
- What are the points of contact I have with them (e.g., formal meetings, informal conversations)?
- What do I need from them to accomplish my goals?
- Are they leaving our interactions with what I want them to have gained?
- Are there any unintended consequences of my interactions with them?

Observing yourself as a leader increases sustainability because leaders do not have to do everything alone. They must build a cohort of committed colleagues who support a shared agenda.

Recognize Routines

Psychologists remind us that about 90 percent of our daily lives is spent in routines. Most habits are positive. You wouldn't want to have to think about how to brush your teeth, put on your shoes, make toast, or drive your car. We learn by practicing the same thing over and over so that eventually the pathways in our brains repeat the sequence without our thinking about it. But sometimes we get into negative routines that thwart our efforts to sustain personal change. The habit of eating cookies and ice cream before bed undermines the goal of losing weight. The routine of surfing the web or spending time on Facebook may hinder the effort to form personal relationships. The habit of playing video games may take away from personal exercise. Before routines can be changed, however, they first must be recognized and scrutinized.

Back in the 1930s, Chester Barnard, an early management guru, talked about "zones of indifference," where people in organizations accept authority and act without conscious thought.[5] He suggested that one of the functions of an executive is to increase the zones of indifference through clear communication and good planning so that employees would accept authority and do the right things. Leaders who attend to zones of indifference shape routines for themselves and others.

Leaders also have routines, or things they do without thinking. Once these routines are identified through the calendar test, they can be adapted. We suggest eight steps in diagnosing and adapting leadership routines:

Step 1: Look at your calendar, and identify the routines that you have. We suggest that you focus on two to four routines that you may want to change.

Step 2: Name each routine. By naming a routine, you give it a label that allows you to talk about, examine, and possibly change it.

Step 3: Figure out where each routine came from. By knowing when and why you started a pattern, you can see if the conditions for it have changed or not.

Step 4: Rate the relevance of the routine for your leadership goals. This overall assessment lets you determine if you want to continue or change the routine.

Steps 5 and 6: Examine the pros and the cons of the routine. The ratio of pro (step 5) to con (step 6) should be about 3:1. That is, you should have at least three reasons to do the routine for every one reason not to do it, or the routine should be further examined and possibly changed.

Step 7: Name a new routine to replace each of the original routines that you've judged ineffective. Again, by naming a new routine, you will make it easier to talk about and more likely to be changed.

Step 8: Outline the first steps at implementing each new routine.

Routines can be recognized, assessed, and modified. Exercise 3.2 sets out the eight steps in a handy grid.

The CEO who desired customer-driven innovation recognized that one of his routines was to begin his day by sitting alone in his office and looking at the financial results of the preceding day. This routine resulted from his past assignments, where he had to monitor daily financial performance. He realized that this routine did not encourage customer innovation because it isolated him from customers and it focused on financial results instead of product innovation. He established a new daily routine that focused on customers. Instead of spending 15 minutes on financial data, he would spend that time developing customer insights. Some days he would look at the firm's share of targeted customers, other days he would call two or three new customers and ask them what led them to use his firm, and still other days he would look at market research to determine future customer trends. The shifts in his routines were not dramatic in terms of personal time, but they sent messages to his organization about what mattered most to him.

Exercise 3.2   Auditing Your Leadership Routines

Step	Routine 1	Routine 2	Routine 3	Routine 4
1. What are some of the routines I do as a leader?				
2. What should I call this routine?				
3. Why do I do this routine? When did it start?				
4. On a scale of 1 (low) to 10 (high), to what extent does this routine help me to reach my goals?				
5. What are the benefits of this routine?				
6. What are the liabilities of this routine?				
7. If I were to change this routine, what would I call the new routine?				
8. What would be the first steps in doing the new routine?				

Replacing dysfunctional with functional routines is not always easy, and old habits tend to creep back. Being conscious about a routine and its negative consequences helps, but it's also necessary to identify trigger events that led to the routine. A leader who scolded employees for poor performance recognized that this behavior happened more when he was surprised by the results in a public forum, where he felt that he had to demonstrate assertive leadership. To sustain his desire to be a more supportive leader, he encouraged subordinates to share negative performance information with him early and privately so that he could digest it before going public. He worked hard to replace his scolding routine with a problem-solving routine in which he could rationally figure out how to fix the poor performance rather than blame someone for it.

See Triggers

When we began our studies in this field as graduate students, our thoughtful advisor, Bill Dyer, taught us to separate underlying symptoms from *presenting problems*—troubles as they first appear. Presenting problems often do not reflect underlying causes or symptoms. We applied this logic when we worked with a manufacturing company that had a relatively high return rate on shipped products. When we explored the underlying causes, we discovered that the company had a strong incentive tied to tracking shipments at the end of each month. Thus, in the last few days of the month, people out to meet their monthly quota would ship products that were not complete or quality tested. They understood that after shipment, they would need to go into the customer workplace to repair the product. We advised the company to change the measurement system so that it rewarded the shipping of products that met quality standards and did not require any on-site rework. Sustained change requires deeper assessment of surface issues and repair of underlying causes.

In business, these triggers show up in predictive analytics, where leaders look for leading indicators of future opportunities. For example, if customer commitment is the goal, a leading indicator is the commitment of employees who interact with customers. A leading indicator of employee commitment is the relationship employees have with their immediate bosses. And a leading indicator of boss-employee relationships is the boss's set of leadership skills and personal insight. This logic creates a line of sight between leadership competencies ("be, know, and do") and customer commitment.

At a personal level, sustaining new habits requires the same exploration of underlying causes. For those working to lose weight, to keep their temper, or to avoid procrastination, it is helpful to explore the underlying causes of weight gain, anger, and dithering. Psychologists often probe these underlying causes by asking, "What does this behavior do for you?" Persistence in ill-conceived behavior generally involves some sort of reward. Unhealthy eating can help to overcome a sense of loneliness, loss of temper with some people can help to avoid conflict with others, and procrastination can be an excuse for an inability to deliver high-quality products. To change a routine often requires honest reflection of what causes the pattern.

Identifying triggers also helps leaders to sustain changes. A leader we coached did a 360-degree review and found that she did not score high on listening to her employees. Before we could help her to improve her listening skills and scores, we had to explore why she did not listen. We generated a number of hypotheses about why someone would score low on listening:

- I don't think that those who work with me have much to contribute to my agenda.
- I have never had a boss who listened to me, and I am doing what I have learned from others.
- I want to listen but don't know how to do it.

- I believe that listening to others takes too much time and keeps me from being effective.
- I tend to be an introvert, and it is difficult for me to spend time with others.

As we discussed possible underlying causes for poor listening scores, we were able to focus on a more sustainable solution to her listening problem. In her case, she felt that her personal style of being an introvert made it difficult for her to listen because she felt uncomfortable with people. With this insight, we were able to talk to her about the differences between predispositions and learned behavior. We pointed out that even if she was predisposed to be an introvert, success in her leadership role required her to learn and demonstrate new behaviors. We reviewed with her the times in her leadership role where she behaved more as an extrovert: doing presentations, running meetings, offering performance feedback. We helped her to realize that while she might be more comfortable working alone without listening to others, in other settings, she had shown the ability to learn to overcome her introverted tendencies because it was a part of her role. We then helped her learn and master some listening skills just as she had learned meeting management skills. Because we explored and worked on the underlying cause of her lack of listening skills, we were able to help her to sustain higher listening scores.

James Claiborn and Cherry Pedrick have explored the process of changing bad habits into good ones.[6] We adapt their work to leaders seeking to replace their dysfunctional with positive behaviors.

Step 1: Describe your leadership behavior. What name would you give it? What is a specific recent example of doing it? How does it feel when you do this behavior?

Step 2: State when the behavior began. When do you first remember doing it?

Step 3: Describe how other people generally respond to this behavior. What happens to those around you when you engage in this behavior? How does that feel to you?

Step 4: Review how the behavior has changed over time. In what ways have you adjusted this behavior?

Step 5: Analyze the triggers for the behavior. Does it generally occur at a usual time of day? Does it generally occur in a particular place or with particular people? What else is going on when this behavior starts?

Step 6: Focus on the triggers, and try to change them. What are the early indicators that you are likely to engage in the behavior? How can you consciously stop the behavior from occurring?

These steps can be adapted to help leaders recognize trigger events that can be overcome to sustain a new behavior.

Start Small and Build to a Tipping Point

In *Tipping Point*, Malcolm Gladwell proposes the *law of accumulation*. For example, when a flu virus hits a tipping point, there is no turning back a full-scale epidemic. This is why health officials try to avoid viruses such as SARS or swine flu and take great precautions to contain them if they appear. However, the idea of creating a tipping point has a real value to leaders who are trying to make change happen.

During the Korean War, the Chinese learned how to get collaboration from American prisoners—a discovery well worth the attention of anyone who intends to create real change, regardless of how repulsive the original effort may seem. They would start small and build on their initial success. Their logic was that if they could get the prisoners to start by doing simple things, they could then get them to move on to more profound things. In one approach, prisoners were asked to go through the following steps:

- Recognize that the United States is not perfect.
- Indicate some of the specific ways that the United States is not perfect.
- Make a list of problems with America.
- Read the list to others.
- Write an essay that discussed these problems in some detail.
- Use the essay with attribution in an anti-American broadcast.

By the time someone had proceeded through these steps, the Chinese had a useful collaborator.

Similar starting-small techniques are embedded into 12-step addiction-recovery programs. These 12-step programs start with small actions, followed by increasingly demanding ones. The first four of the original 12 steps as published by Alcoholics Anonymous focused on self-reflection:

1. We admitted we were powerless over alcohol—that our lives had become unmanageable.
2. We came to believe that a power greater than ourselves could restore us to sanity.
3. We made a decision to turn our will and our lives over to the care of God *as we understood Him.*
4. We made a searching and fearless moral inventory of ourselves.

The last four steps require much more public and demanding behavior change:

9. We made direct amends to such people wherever possible, except when to do so would injure them or others.
10. We continued to take personal inventory and when we were wrong promptly admitted it.
11. We sought through prayer and meditation to improve our conscious contact with God *as we understood Him,* praying only for knowledge of His will for us and the power to carry that out.

12. Having had a spiritual awakening as the result of these steps, we tried to carry this message to alcoholics and to practice these principles in all our affairs.

Starting small builds success and leads to more success. At the heart of the 12-step programs is the adage "one day at a time"—meaning that you only have to change the behavior for one day. Then, when tomorrow comes, you do it again. This approach avoids the sort of "I have to do this forever" mind-set that automatically triggers resistance.

The cumulative effect of small changes adding up to substantive change shows up in economics, where individuals are invited to save a small percentage of their money on a regular basis; in physiology, where exercise begins with what someone can do; and in the "broken-windows theory" of managing crime, where police go after small crimes and not just the big ones. As the Chinese philosopher Lao-tzu said about 600 BC, "[A] journey of a thousand miles begins with a single step."

To build sustainable change, effective leaders start with small and simple changes that show up on their forward-looking calendar. When we work with leaders, we brainstorm 8 to 10 things they could do to help reach their desired outcome. We then ask them to prioritize the first two or three based on two questions: Which of these actions are most ...

- Easy for you to implement?
- Likely to have a big payback?

These two questions drive what we call the *payoff matrix* (shown in Figure 3.1). We used this matrix in helping to change an organization culture in a program called "Work-Out" at General Electric and in coaching individual leaders to focus on quick wins to get started with change.[7]

Figure 3.1   Payoff matrix.

		Implementability	
		Easy to Implement	Tough to Implement
Payoff	Small payoff	Quick win	Time wasters
	Big payoff	Business opportunity	Special effort

To ensure progress in the quick-win quadrant, we rely on what we call the *15-minute drill*. When a leader makes a commitment to a desired change, we ask, What will you do in 15 minutes in the next few days to show that you are committed to this new behavior? Anyone can find 15 minutes per day over the next two or three days if they have any interest at all in changing. For the CEO desiring customer innovation, these actions included such things as scheduling a meeting with key customers and R&D experts, reviewing a report on industry trends, and changing the agenda for key staff meetings to focus on customer innovation. Sustainability comes because small actions generate momentum until they reach a tipping point as the leader gains confidence through early successes.

Manage Signals and Symbols

Classic Greek plays relied on melodrama to exaggerate the meaning of a story to appeal to the emotions of the audience, but individual actions often do have meaning far beyond the action itself. In Chapter 2 we cited Martin Luther King's classic "I have a dream" speech. The fact that he gave this rousing address about freedom while standing in front of the Lincoln Memorial reinforced his message. When John Kennedy announced his bold plan for a "man on the moon in this decade," it was before a special joint session of Congress. This was the only joint session of Congress in his presidency other than his required inauguration and state of the union addresses, making the message even more symbolic and prominent. President Reagan's "tear down this wall" comment was at the Brandenburg Gate near the Berlin wall, a location that symbolized his commitment to end the cold war. After September 11, George Bush returned to the White House to communicate to the American people and then spoke again on September 14 from Ground Zero.

Leaders sustain change by paying attention to the signals and symbols of their actions. This occurs in advertising, where Apple has portrayed its users as cool, fashionable, and trendy through their dress, language, and style—as compared with an image of Microsoft as stodgy, rigid, and disconnected. Leadership symbols shape how the public responds to the leader, for good or ill. When Tony Hayward, the CEO of BP, arrived at the site of the Gulf of Mexico oil leak disaster, he walked on the beach wearing formal clothes and said, "There's no one who wants this over more than I do. I would like my life back." By making the disaster about himself, and by looking like a stiff business executive, he signaled his insensitivity to the enormity of the disaster and its impact on others.

Leadership symbolism is not just about the leader's time but also about where the message is delivered, how it is delivered, and what the leader communicates through looks and actions. The CEO we worked with wanted to visit his key customers. In the past, CEO visits were formal events where he would visit with the CEO of his customer and review the company's needs and his firm's products and services. Since he wanted to signal a commitment to real innovation and customer responsiveness, he changed the way he made his visits. He decided to follow the flow of his product through the customer engagement process to learn what could be improved at each step of the way. He began in the customer's purchasing department asking questions about how the buyers assessed his product against its competitors. This experience taught him about how to better differentiate his product. He then spent time in the warehouse and on the dock with workers who received his product and discovered how to improve its packaging. Then he went to the manufacturing and assembly unit to learn how to improve his product's fit with the customer's product. Finally, he met with the CEO and chief financial officer (CFO) to learn how to price and market the product. This revised customer tour led to unique insights about each stage of customer engagement. He also signaled a willingness to partner with the customer to innovate and integrate his work so that he could gain customer share.

Leaders who attend to signals and symbols pay attention to issues such as these:

- *Physical appearance.* What messages do my clothing and looks send to those with whom I work? In a business offsite, we worked with a leader who showed up unshaven, in very casual dress, and with uncombed hair. He was trying to communicate a sense of comfort and casualness, but his dishevelment sent a message of not taking the offsite seriously. There is a time and place for either formal or informal attire. Political leaders quickly learn that always wearing a white shirt, tie, and suit distances them from their constituents. They learn to wear casual clothes to better connect with their audiences.
- *Physical setting.* What are the settings where I do my work? Effective leaders pay attention to where they meet (e.g., in their own office or in others' offices) and the settings in which they meet (e.g., in a formal boardroom or in a smaller breakout room). We have coached leaders who wanted to signal willingness to listen to others to simply say, "Let me come to your office for this meeting." Leaders who say "we want to collaborate with you" but then force others to always come to their office are not really expressing collaboration behaviors.
- *Office architecture.* How does my office reflect my desired leadership style and behavior? Most workplaces, whether they are cubicles or formal offices, send messages about what matters to the leader.

Is the office clean or cluttered? What pictures are on the wall? What books are on the selves? What are the colors? Where do people sit? One leader would consistently sit behind his desk when meeting with employees, who were on the other side of the desk. This sent a message of formality and distance. His successor replaced the formal desk with a small table so that the leader was knee to knee with those with whom he met.

- *Personal choices.* How do my personal choices signal my priorities? We worked with a CEO who was a third-generation leader of a successful family company. As a result of his heritage and position, he was very wealthy. He drove to work in a red Ferrari and had pictures of his yacht throughout his office. Another leader who founded a company and was very wealthy drove to work in a more modest car and did not talk about or show pictures of his yacht. In both cases, the leaders were affluent, and employees knew it. In the first case, the leader distanced himself from those he led; in the second case, the leader put himself in a position to relate to others more effectively.

Time is not simply what leaders do; it is the whole context of how and where they spend it. As leaders pay attention to the subtle and not-so-subtle choices they make, they signal a commitment to sustainable change.

Be Consistent

Consistency is the ultimate time challenge. Often behavior changes are events, not patterns. We do something for a short period, but it does not endure. In Chapter 1 we talked about how difficult it is to sustain personal change. Recidivism occurs when efforts to overcome bad habits fail. The recidivism rates for released prisoners in the United States have been estimated at about 60 percent compared with 50 percent in the United Kingdom.[8] The U.S. Department of Justice tracked the arrests, convictions, and incarcerations of former inmates for three years after their release from prisons in 15 states. These showed that released prisoners with the highest arrest rates were robbers (70.2 percent), burglars (74.0 percent), larcenists (74.6 percent), motor vehicle thieves (78.8 percent), those in prison for possessing or selling stolen property (77.4 percent), and those in prison for possessing, using, or selling illegal weapons (70.2 percent).[9] Likewise, relapse rates for drug-related addictive diseases usually are in the range of 50 to 90 percent. These rates vary by definition of relapse, severity of addiction, which drug of addiction, length of treatment, gender, and elapsed time from treatment discharge to assessment, as well as other factors.[10]

While such relapses show a lack of sustainable change for extremely addictive behaviors, consistent changes have occurred in some cases. For instance, U.S. seat belt use has increased dramatically[11]:

1984: 14%	1993: 66%	2002: 75%
1985: 21%	1994: 67%	2003: 79%
1986: 37%	1995: 68%	2004: 80%
1987: 42%	1996: 68%	2005: 82%
1988: 45%	1997: 69%	2006: 81%
1989: 46%	1998: 69%	2007: 82%
1990: 49%	1999: 67%	2008: 83%
1991: 59%	2000: 71%	2009: 84%
1992: 62%	2001: 73%	2010: 85%

There are no simple reasons for this consistent change, but most of us who ride in a car now automatically put on seat belts. It has become a natural act. The increased consistency of seat belt use likely comes from an onslaught of information about the benefits of wearing seat belts ("Seat belts save lives"), more comfortable seat belts that are easier to use (shoulder harnesses), reminders (the beeping when we don't wear them), and reinforcement (tickets for not wearing them). Consistency is generally made up of lots of small triggers.

As noted earlier, we encourage the leaders we coach to pick a behavior they want to improve and then turn the desired behavior into actions that show up in their calendar. Many leaders treat these actions as experiments, not commitments. Commitments require consistency and endurance with the new behavior until it becomes a new routine. Our colleague Steve Kerr suggests that in many training programs leaders learn new ideas and even practice behaviors related to those ideas. But he calls this "an unnatural act (a new behavior) in an unnatural place (a training or coaching session)." Sustainability does not occur until the new behavior becomes a natural act (a routine or pattern) in a natural place (the work setting).

Consistency replaces leadership hypocrisy with sincerity and authenticity. Over time, even skeptical employees recognize and accept the leader's new behavior if it is consistent. To help leaders build consistency, we use a tool called the *four 3s:*

Three hours. We encourage leaders to identify what they can do immediately—in the first three hours—to turn an idea into an action that may take only 15 minutes.

Three days. The behavior becomes a little more comfortable and recognizable if they can do it for three days. This means that the leader needs to calendar forward by figuring out who he or she will talk with or meet with, what he or she will say and do, and how he or she will do it on each of the next three days.

Three weeks. Doing the same behavior for three weeks begins to feel like a habit. In the 1960s, Maxwell Maltz brought together cognitive-behavioral therapy and cybernetics research to help people reach their goals.[12] In particular, as a medical doctor, he studied how to help amputees realign their expectations and adjust to their new circumstances. He came up with the rationale for a 21-day commitment. He proposed that in 21 days of consistent repeated use, the brain forms engrams that connect neurologically. He found that an average patient would show remarkable progress as a result.[12] By visualization and concrete action for 21 days, individuals change their self-concept. His thinking and research became the foundation for many self-help gurus (e.g., Zig Ziglar, Tony Robbins, and Brian Tracy) who propose 21-day self-improvement plans. We suggest to leaders than they practice their desired behavior every day for 21 days to change their routines. Leaders need to practice their new behavior every day, and it works best if they do the behavior at the same time every day. We also recommend that leaders write their expectations to document how they are doing and what they are learning. Putting intentions into writing increases self-reflection, which reinforces the ideas and promotes learning.

Three months. To become fully consistent, leaders not only need to change their personal behavior, but they also need to get others to recognize, accept, and expect the behavior. Leaders at this point may publicly talk about the changes they have intended and accomplished. After 90 days, leaders change expectations others have of them, which is a huge source of reinforcement.

It is hard to resist the tendency to see yourself as others see you, so efforts to change the way others see you pay off in improved sustainability. When leaders consistently behave as if they are committed, they will be committed. In our CEO case, after three months of consistently acting to identify and serve customers, employees began to expect it. New employees who had not experienced him as COO primarily identified him as a customer-focused leader. This external validation sustained his internal identity. His intent now matched his behavior. He was no longer a hypocrite. He was a strong CEO with a credible agenda to increase customer-driven innovation, and he already had some small wins under his belt.

The four 3s help leaders' time to become a consistent reflection of their intentions. Exercise 3.3 provides a worksheet to help you get started.

Exercise 3.3   Creating Time Consistency Through the Four 3s

Time	Question	Actions	Application for Me
3 hours	What can I do in the next three hours to demonstrate my desired changed?	Start with small actions: 15-minute drill.	
3 days	In the next three days, how will my calendar reflect my intentions?	Practice the new behavior every day.	
3 weeks	How do I maintain my new behavior for 21 days?	Calendar forward so that the new behavior shows up in what you do, who you do it with, where you do it, and how you do it.	
3 months	How does my new behavior become an expectation others have of me?	Go public with your new behavior so that others expect it of you.	

Conclusion: Leaders as Time Loggers

We began this chapter with the leadership sustainability challenge of turning expectations into actions. These actions overcome leadership hypocrisy when leaders do what they say. By gaining discipline over time and mastering the seven principles we suggest, leaders ultimately forge a new identity. As their identity becomes accepted and expected, they are more able to sustain new leadership behaviors and deliver the results they desire.

iphone: **RedLaser**
Android: **Barcode Scanner**

Scan this QR code to watch a video about time management.

leadershipsustainability.com/ qr/time

CHAPTER 4

ACCOUNTABILITY

4

The man who complains about the way the ball bounces is
likely to be the one who dropped it.

—Lou Holtz

The need for accountability applies in many parts of life. Politicians
who make promises they don't keep quickly lose the confidence of
their electorate. Primary and secondary schools that fail to prepare
students for university hinder education and limit the workforce. Public
servants who encourage or depend on bribes and corruption undermine
government's ability to serve citizens. At a personal level, we are accountable to our partners, children, friends, and associates. Accountability
leads to trust. Trust leads to improved relationships. Improved relationships on the job lead to more referrals and better collaboration. More
referrals and better collaboration lead to sustained performance.

Real-Life Accountability

Here are two leaders who strengthened their companies and their
own leadership by attending to accountability.

Peter Loescher, CEO of Siemens

Peter Loescher was brought into Siemens as CEO in July 2007 after a
corruption scandal rocked the huge Germany-based conglomerate to its

core. Siemens employs 360,000 people in nearly 190 countries. Loescher was the twelfth CEO and the first outsider to lead the 165-year-old company. Change in a company this size is always difficult and even more so for an outsider, but Loescher was up to the task.

Loescher acted fast to ingrain accountability into the culture of Siemens and did not miss the opportunity to use the crisis to the company's benefit. Before Loescher became CEO, Siemens was run by a complex set of intertwined "circulars" or committees in charge of the businesses. These committees reported to other committees. When a decision reached an impasse, yet another committee was formed to resolve it. The heads of these committees were referred to as "coaches," implying their purpose as facilitators rather than as the people responsible and accountable for delivering results.

On his first day in office, Loescher changed this bureaucratic committee structure and sponsored the "CEO principle," which guides Siemens today. The CEO principle is made up of simple statements that drive accountability throughout the company:

1. Decisions are ultimately the responsibility of an individual.
2. Leaders need a line of sight to make effective decisions.
3. Leaders must be willing to take individual accountability for their actions.
4. Key placement decisions are benchmarked with outside leaders.

To institutionalize this shift in culture and to signal that the old ways would not return, Loescher replaced 90 percent of the managing board, 70 percent of the leaders at the second level, and 50 percent of leaders at the third level within three years. This was the end of the old guard and demonstrated that Loescher would not tolerate leaders who did not follow his agenda.

Through this process, Loescher has transformed Siemens' culture and its results. The company has increased market share, tripled capital efficiency, and is growing. Decisions are made faster, and Siemens' people are closer to their customers than ever before. This accountability philosophy in action attracts a completely different kind of leader and employee to the company, forming a virtuous cycle that enables ongoing success.

Matt Holland, President, Utah Valley University

Matt Holland grew up as the son of a university president, so it was not a complete surprise that he entered academics. He completed a Ph.D. in political science at Duke University, worked as a consultant at Monitor Group, and began teaching. He had not intended to pursue an academic administrative career, but when he was invited to Utah Valley University (UVU), he felt compelled to help the community tackle the challenge of meeting the needs of one of the fastest-growing universities in the nation. With this prompting, he applied for and was chosen as the sixth president of the university in 2009.

UVU, with an enrollment of more than 33,000, serves students primarily from the Orem and Provo areas of Utah. It started out as an open-enrollment college with a strong orientation toward technical and applied degrees, eventually offering approximately 60 bachelor degrees, more than 60 associate degrees, and more than 20 certificate and diploma programs. In 2008, it shifted from college to university status and has become the largest open-enrollment university in Utah (and one of the largest in the United States).

When Holland arrived, he felt that he would need to articulate a vision for the university. But what he found was a plethora of vision statements. As in many other university cultures, committees and councils ran UVU with extensive faculty participation. Each council created its own vision of the university. Instead of creating another new vision, Holland felt that he needed to synthesize the existing ones into consistent themes that would integrate and shape the overall university direction. With input from the leadership team, four themes emerged:

- *Inclusive.* UVU provides opportunities for individuals from a wide variety of backgrounds and perspectives and meets regional educational needs.
- *Engaged.* UVU engages its communities in mutually beneficial collaboration and emphasizes engaged learning.
- *Serious.* UVU fosters a culture of academic rigor and professional excellence.
- *Student success.* UVU supports students in achieving their educational, professional, and personal goals.

As these four themes became a focus of the university, Holland realized that the real challenge was to make them more than rhetoric—to have them shape behaviors and actions within the university, that is, to build accountability to them.

To make sustained progress on his four themes, Holland created an accountability process for both personal leadership and the organization. He personally modeled the process by publicly talking about his five top presidential priorities, linking each of those priorities to the four major themes and committing to publicly reporting on his progress one year later. He asked each member of his presidential council to follow the same process (i.e., publicly stating top priorities, linking them to themes, and reporting back a year later) for themselves and for their staff. By cascading personal accountability throughout the organization, Holland helped leaders to set goals related to the themes and report on them a year later.

To institutionalize the process throughout the university, Holland asked the university planning council to set two to four objectives for each theme and then to define indicators for each of those objectives. These themes, objectives, and indicators are then published and shared throughout the university. This planning process has evolved to an annual cycle of planning, budgeting, doing, and reviewing. The results are shared widely inside the university as well as outside with accreditors, legislators, and community stakeholders.

Who, Me?

Recently, one of our two-year-old granddaughters ate some of the cookies that her mother had prepared for dessert. When asked whether she had eaten the cookies, she looked away, glanced around, and quietly said, "Who, me?"

In a two-year-old, this is cute. In a leader, it is not.

Accountability must occur in both thought and action for leaders. At the personal level, accountability deals with ensuring that leaders keep their word and do what they say they will do. Leaders also increase individual accountability throughout the workforce by finding ways to motivate and engage employees. At the organization level, accountability increases when leaders create systems and practices that focus, drive, and reinforce employee behaviors and organization actions.

A failure of leadership accountability produces bad outcomes. Hosni Mubarak, the toppled Egyptian dictator, arrived in court on a stretcher and was charged with killing pro-democracy protesters during the Arab Spring revolts. Lying on his stretcher in his white prison overalls, the 83-year-old entered his plea: "I deny all these charges and accusations categorically," he said. Mubarak is accused of economic corruption, illegal business deals involving gas exports to Israel, and killing protesters during the 18-day uprising against his regime.

Amnesty International and other human rights organizations warn that Mubarak's prosecution must be conducted fairly. "This trial represents a historic opportunity for Egypt to hold a former leader and his inner circle to account for crimes committed during their rule," said Malcolm Smart, Amnesty director for the Middle East and North Africa. Without a fair trial, the newly defined government lacks accountability to due process.[1]

People expect leaders to be accountable and to at least have the intent of making correct choices. When that doesn't happen, stakeholders feel violated. It's a scam when someone who should be accountable is not. Any leader who expects sustainable results must ensure personal and organizational accountability.

In doing performance appraisals, sometimes employees think that the appraisal is for the appraiser not the appraisee. One leader reported that at the end of a performance discussion, an employee said, "Thanks for sharing the information with me. You have done a good job helping me know how I am doing." The leader needed to help the employee realize that the purpose of the appraisal was not for the leader but for the employee. With coaching and training, the leader responded to the employee, "What have you learned, and how will you apply that learning?"

Leaders build accountability in others and for themselves through four principles of accountability:

- Take personal responsibility.
- Go public.
- Be consistent with your personal values and brand.
- Hold others accountable.

Take Personal Responsibility

The most difficult part of taking personal responsibility is resisting the urge to blame others for our problems. Linda Galindo tells the following story:

Suppose a husband and wife work at exactly the same job. As they walk out of the house together in the morning, Husband believes that 60 percent of the success of the day's work belongs to him, and 40 percent depends on outside conditions: the boss's mood; how often the telephone rings; whether he gets a flat tire on the way to work; how well he slept the night before.

Wife, on the other hand, is consciously committed to having a successful day. She believes that 85 percent of her success depends on her, and just 15 percent could be motivated by outside sources.

It should come as no surprise when, over dinner that evening, Wife has a happier day to recount than does Husband.

Here's why:

She chose to ignore the boss's bad mood, or she simply accepted his crankiness and found a way to engage him in the task at hand.

She chose not to answer the telephone for two hours so she could work without interruptions and finish her project more quickly.

Because she slept poorly the night before, she chose to compensate by taking a brisk walk at lunchtime instead of sitting in the too-warm cafeteria, becoming over-relaxed and eating the comfort foods that she knows can make her sleepy....

She chose before she left the house in the morning to be responsible—at least 85 percent of the way—for the success of her own day. ...

The mind-set to be responsible can be measured on a scale that ranges from 0 to 100 percent.

The higher the percentage of ownership you believe you have when you begin your day, a project, or your job, the more success you'll have.[2]

We like the idea of an 85 percent solution for taking personal responsibility. Clearly, some things are outside our control—but even with those, we can choose how we respond. Victor Frankl's experience in a prisoner of war camp showed that how we interpret our conditions has more impact on our well-being than the conditions themselves.

Use I Statements and We Statements

A tool that helps us to take personal responsibility is to use *I* statements and *we* statements at the right time and under the right circumstances. When you are about to blame someone else, turn the blame statement into an *I* statement. When you are about to take credit for something, use a *we* statement. When you become aware of the subtle differences between these two types of statements, you may notice that you have used one at the wrong time. We blame instead of taking personal responsibility, and we take credit instead of sharing credit. Table 4.1 compares the two for various situations.

Leaders who take personal responsibility use *I* statements and *we* statements in ways that garner support for what is being done. With practice, they get better at using the right statement at the right time by focusing on results and sustainability rather than taking credit or assigning blame. A leader who takes personal responsibility is easier to be around, and others want to help.

In performance reviews, when leaders miss goals, they often like to blame the business setting, other people, or unforeseen conditions. They are more likely to make desired improvements when they recognize headwinds but have a no-excuses attitude. We have found that leaders gain enormous personal credit and make real progress when they admit failures, missed goals, or mistakes that others probably already know. When facing a mistake, we encourage leaders to (1) acknowledge the mistake by simply declaring what went wrong, (2) take personal responsibility for it by saying that they recognize their part in the mistake and

Table 4.1   Taking Responsibility and Sharing Credit

Blame Statement—"It's your fault"	I Statement—"It's my responsibility"
"You made us late because you didn't set your alarm."	"I should have called to wake you up this morning when I saw how late it was getting."
"You talked too much during the presentation and turned off the client."	"I did not set up a premeeting so that we could practice how to approach this client and get our roles clarified."
"Your presentation had so many errors that it made us look like idiots."	"I left too little time to rehearse the presentation and work out the bugs."
Me Statement—Taking Credit	*We* Statement—Sharing Credit
"I think I bowled over that group with my fascinating examples and compelling style."	"We bowled over that group, and your help with the presentation was crucial."
"I'm pretty sure we will get the sale. I really nailed it with a superior understanding of their industry based on my previous experience."	"We got the sale. Our team's homework led to the insights that made a difference."
"My contribution to this meeting was far more valuable than yours."	"Let's use the meeting time to share what we each do well."

regret it, (3) share lessons learned by disclosing what they learned and will do differently in the future, and (4) ask for support by inviting others to help them not make the same mistake again. It is unwise to "run and hide" because the mistake will recur. It is wiser to be transparent by running into the mistake and being transparent about how to resolve it.

Foster the Right Attitude

One of our business school professors, Phil Daniels, told his classes, "Your attitude determines your altitude"—and his message still resonates. Leaders who deliver sustainable results stand out from other leaders in their attitude toward work and others.

In a recent HBR blog, Anthony Tjan asserted that attitude is what determines business luck. "We have found in our research that people who self-describe themselves as lucky in their entrepreneurial profile with us tend to be luckier because they have the right attitude."[3] This attitude stems from three traits:

- *Humility.* A balance between self-confidence and understanding of limitations.
- *Intellectual curiosity.* An intense drive to learn more about just about anything that leads to meeting new people, asking new questions, and going to new places.
- *Optimism.* A belief that more, better, and faster are always possible.

Leaders who are accountable embrace the possibility of full personal responsibility. While others try to be right and to get credit, these leaders have a "lucky" attitude about mistakes and getting others to sustain what they want. Their attitude determines their altitude. They have a humility borne of experience that everyone makes mistakes and that walking into mistakes and acknowledging their flaws helps people to see them as more credible not less.

Mike Ulrich, Dave's son, has a great attitude about mistakes. Mike worked as a statistician and research associate with our consulting firm, RBL Group, for a year while he applied to various Ph.D. programs. Given the economic recession, many more students than normal are applying to doctoral programs, so competition is very stiff for a limited number of spots. Mike decided not to hide his rejection letters from various schools. He posted the letters on his office door in full public view of anyone walking down the hall. Because he did this, the entire firm became invested in his success. He soon received some acceptance letters, and they excited everyone. We were enrolled in Mike's acceptance to a good school. By embracing his failure (by way of the rejection letters), Mike's attitude encouraged success. This year he has taken this attitude of accountability to the University of South Carolina, where he is on his way to receiving a Ph.D.

We have been invited to coach leaders when they have made mistakes that could impair their careers. One of the signs that help us to recognize people ready to sustain change is the way they deal with such mistakes. Some leaders want to do all they can to avoid the issue—they won't bring it up, and they change the subject or find excuses if someone else does. These leaders avoid accountability and are not likely to sustain change. Other leaders run toward the problem. They talk about it as objectively as they can and ask for ideas on how they could have improved. They have enough confidence to admit that they made a mistake, learned from it, and moved on.

Go Public

If you really want to hold yourself accountable, tell people what you intend. Go public. When leaders go public with their goals, they are more likely to stick with them. One leader told us that when he announced goals, he always tried to avoid providing a lifeboat that would allow him to renege on his commitments. There are many ways to go public.

One high-tech company was losing some of its top talent, particularly those who had been at the company three to seven years. It put in place a policy that the highest-rated talent would spend three weeks per year on campus recruiting. It was an honor to be selected to do the campus recruiting because it sent a signal to the organization of being a high performer. But even more, when these technical stars presented the benefits of working at the company, they not only attracted future employees, but they also recommitted themselves. The firm found a nearly 100 percent retention level of those who went public with their positive recruiting message.

In a similar vein, many companies use referral hiring, where employees refer peers to join the company. Most such programs focus on who is referred, but it is better to focus on who does the referring. By referring a colleague to work for the company, an employee goes public with a commitment to the company. We have advised taking referrals only from high-performing employees because getting a referral accepted will tend to add to the commitment of the person who made it.

When presenting a proposal, speaking to employees, connecting with customers, or communicating with investors, leaders should be aware of who presents almost as much as what is presented. When individuals go public with their commitment to the firm, they end up more likely to sustain their commitment.

Sustainable commitment increases when you go public to someone you trust and respect. For years, at workshops we would have participants prepare an action plan of what they would do and then share it with someone in the room, often a stranger. Now we ask participants to synthesize what they have learned and what they will do and send a text or e-mail to someone they know at work or home who will follow up with them. These unexpected texts or e-mails inevitably will create a subsequent conversation that helps the participant to go public with his or her desired improvements. By using technology in the classroom, we have helped leaders to go public with their commitments. In one company, we asked the senior leaders in a workshop to plan a one-hour staff meeting the morning of the last day of the workshop. On that morning, we had each of the participants in the workshop do a phone conference with his or her staff to share what the participant had learned and how it might affect his or her work going forward. Again, the principle is that when leaders go public with a commitment, it is more likely to be sustained.

Lean manufacturing has been used to improve work processes for many companies. At the heart of lean is public reporting of how work is done. If you walk through a lean facility, there are whiteboards with hourly, shift, or daily results that employees constantly update. These public reports keep people focused on the goals and committed to reaching them.

At the senior levels of a company, we have encouraged leaders to go public with their goals in webinars, videos, newsletters, and external media campaigns. The more a leader publicly commits to a course of action, the more likely that course of action is to be sustained.

Reality television has captured this principle. In *Airline*, a show recorded in 2004 and 2005, Southwest Airlines pilots, flight attendants, and airport employees were profiled as they heard heartwarming passenger stories and experienced occasional outbursts, weather-related anxiety, and heightened security measures—all while trying to meet everyone's urgent timetable. The company's confidence in going public with a demanding customer-service business helped workers to face and improve their service. (A new show, *On the Fly*, returned Southwest to the airwaves in 2012.) *Undercover Boss* invites a senior leader to go into disguise for a week as a novice employee and then to go public with the lessons learned. These shows build on the go-public principle by asking employees and leaders to be transparent with their work.

Be Consistent with Personal Values and Brand

Leaders sustain change when the change is consistent with their personal values. Value consistency helps leaders to think and act with continuity so that their stance and actions are clear both to themselves and to observers. To ensure consistency of personal values, we often invite leaders to prepare a statement that reflects their personal point of view about leadership. These personal points of view consider a number of issues, such as what leaders believe, how they aspire to behave, and who they are and want to become.

To create this point of view, we often show film clips of inspiring leaders such as Martin Luther King, and then we invite participants to craft their personal vision. The leaders define who they are, what matters most to them, and where they are going. The exercise results in leadership visions, missions, aspirations, and points of view.

We now recognize that these efforts do not fully drive leadership sustainability. Leaders who are more self-aware may have personal insight and intensity, but unless they are directed in the right ways, they won't have sustainable impact. To have sustainable impact, *a leadership point of view needs to become a personal leader brand.* We suggest three elements to building this personal brand to be consistent with your values:

- A personal brand focuses outside first and then inside.
- A personal brand is carried through experience and story.
- A personal brand is sustainable.

External Focus

Most work in leadership starts by looking inward. Most of the leadership points of view we hear begin with *I* statements:

I believe…
I aspire to…
I want…
I hope…
I will…

These personal statements have passion and purpose. They are meaningfully read and shared. But they are incomplete and not sustainable. The brand metaphor focuses on the outside, not the inside. Brand value shows up in the mind of the customer. The pizzazz of Apple, the experience of Disney, the "third good place" of Starbucks, the connection of Nokia, and the quality of Toyota are all brand identities that communicate to customers and investors. Brand power comes from the outside in.

A leadership point of view is generally internally focused; it's about who I am as a leader. A personal leader brand is externally focused; it's about how my leadership impacts others. When a crisis hits, a leader with a personal point of view focuses inside to get grounded on values, strengths, and style. This leader has authenticity and emotional intelligence to handle the crisis. In a crisis, though, a leader with a personal leader brand perspective asks how the crisis will affect others: What is the impact of the crisis on employees, customers, investors, and communities? This leader's job is to make sure that the response to the crisis serves these stakeholders. The external focus determines the right thing to do, and the inside perspective is about having the character and energy to do the right thing the right way. Both inside and outside perspectives matter, but the sequence has more accountability by going outside first and then inside.

By focusing outside first, leaders make sure that their point of view will be of benefit to someone else. Sometimes leaders may have a point of view founded on their strengths, but unless they strengthen others, they will not be as valuable or as sustainable as they could be. The outside-in focus is also more sustainable because it gains commitment from others, not just from oneself.

In a recent workshop, leaders were asked to write their personal points of view. One of these statements stood out as more reflective of a personal leader brand:

As a leader, I am here *to be of service to others* and in the service of a meaningful purpose. In the context of financial services, I am inspired by the risks our organization continues to take to deliver greater transparency and value *to our customers*, to shift the accepted ethical boundaries *of our industry*. I believe there is always a better way to do business, and superior returns will come with *our customers' interests at heart.* Within this context, I hope to be recognized as a leader with courage, who puts the *interests of her team and the organization before her own.* I strive to make the decisions that are *right for others,* regardless of my personal imperatives. (italics added)

Note that the writer focuses less on herself and more on the service she provides to others. Her identity is not from the inside out but from the outside in, and thus we believe that she will be able to sustain it. She has created expectations from others of who she will be and what she will do, and that will help her to keep to her goals.

Leaders may strive to acquire personal strengths of authenticity, judgment, emotional intelligence, credibility, and other noble attributes. However, following the outside-in logic of brand building, without applying these strengths in ways that create value for others, it is not possible to create a personal leader brand.

Experience and Story

A leadership point of view offers insights into and perspectives on what the leader needs to know and do. A personal brand offers a story that captures not only what is known and done but also the emotion and feeling behind it. Brand has an emotional pull that sends a signal of what matters. We wear branded clothing not simply to be clothed but also to send a message about who we are. We drive a branded car to communicate our identity, not for basic transportation. Most brands tell a story. The Mont Blanc pen we use is a gift from a friend. When we use the pen, we remember the friend more than the pen. A brand has a personal and public story.

Leaders who shift from a point of view to a personal brand do more than discuss what they should know and do; they move on to what they feel and value and, ultimately, to who they are. Their personal leader brand offers a narrative about their identity and thus becomes more sustainable.

In helping companies craft a firm brand that reflects their culture, we often ask the question, What are the top three things your company wants to be known for in the future by your best customers? The responses to this question shift strategy, mission, and vision statements into firm brand and organization culture. Likewise, we have asked leaders a similar question: What are the top three things you as a leader want to be known for in the future by those you lead? This question is not just about what the leader knows and does; it is about the identity the leader hopes to create in the minds of the led. This identity forms the leadership story that plays out to shape a personal brand narrative.

Sustainability

Brands have impact beyond any single quarterly period, product, or advertising campaign. Lasting brands endure because they are patterns, not events. And rhetoric and design are not enough; organization brands emerge from many consistent actions over time that communicate and embed a brand promise. Brand recall comes when the brand endures over time and place.

We see too many leadership points of view that are more rhetoric than resolve, more aspiration than action, and more hopeful than real. Brand promises without subsequent results are not sustained. Leadership wish lists need to be replaced with leadership vows. When we ask leaders to prepare their personal brand, they are making commitments about what they have to do to sustain their personal brand in the eyes of those they serve. A brand focus builds sustainability through accountability.

Personal leader brand means that noble ideas are linked to daily behavior. Personal leader brand focuses on the way simple actions influence and make a difference in long-term results. Personal leader brand requires personal passion coupled with interpersonal awareness and a commitment to constant learning. Personal leader brand builds on personal values as they create value for others. Personal leader brand endures over time.

Hold Others Accountable

Building personal responsibility, going public, and shaping personal brand develop sustainability through individual accountability. But sustainability also comes when others are accountable. By holding others accountable, leaders also become more personally accountable for sustaining their desired changes through four phases:

1. Set clear objectives.
2. Identify measures.
3. Ensure consequences.
4. Provide ongoing feedback and follow up.

Leaders who use these four phases sequentially ensure accountability in both themselves and others. Sometimes leaders make mistakes by skipping one of the phases. For example, some leaders try to build creative incentives (in the consequences phase) without having clear measures. If it is unclear what is expected, it is difficult to enforce consequences. Likewise, it is difficult to have measures without objectives.

Set Clear Objectives

Leaders cannot be personally accountable or hold others accountable to ambiguous objectives. If it is not clear what is expected, we never know how well we are doing. Setting clear objectives leading to accountability involves six elements that we call the *ABC's* (actually *ABCDEF*):

Aspiration
Behavior
Customer connectivity
Discipline
Energy (or emotion)
Focus

Aspiration

Clear objectives envision a future state that defines what can be, not just an extension of what has been. A leader establishes an aspirational objective by creating a mental image of what might be. To be sustainable, the aspiration should exceed resources, but not so far as to create cynicism. We were once in a firm where leaders stated a bold aspiration—"to have $15 billion in sales in 2015." Unfortunately, the path from the present $7 billion to the aspirational $15 billion level was unclear. Employees did not think they could accomplish it, so they shrugged and went on with business as usual. At the other end of the scale, leaders define a future state primarily as an extension of the present and miss what a new future might look like—$15 billion might have been incomprehensible, but $7.5 billion would have been dull. To lead to sustainable accountability, aspirations need to be distinctive, showing how the organization is uniquely positioned to define a future state.

Behavior

Aspirational objectives need to be translated into employee behaviors. In Chapter 3 we talked about the way priorities show up in how employees spend time: the things they do, the people they meet with, the place they work, and the way they get work done. Absent a focus on behavior, aspirations inspire but don't endure. Leaders shape aspirations, but employees specify behaviors. The best way to build a shared aspiration is to present the initial ideas interactively, allowing employees to respond to them and define what specific things they could do more or less of in the next month to implement the vision. This invariably gets better results than a one-way forum where the leader speaks and the employees take notes.

Customer Connectivity

An important test for a sustainable objective is to ask, How would our target customers respond to this? This test helps you to reframe internally focused business shorthand (i.e., service, quality, and low cost) in terms of goals that matter to external customers. Service might mean answering phones within four rings, resolving customer problems within 24 hours, or having a personal contact with target customers each quarter. When customers want and define the outcomes you pursue, what you do is more likely to be a direct benefit for your business.

Discipline

Objectives require organization processes that align with the aspiration. Programs such as Six Sigma, reengineering, and manufacturing excellence offer disciplines to make an aspiration real. To have sustainable accountability, leaders who draft aspirations should follow up quickly with initiatives that validate the objective. These disciplines consume resources, but they also communicate commitment in a way that makes them well worthwhile.

Energy (or Emotion)

Aspirational objectives inspire people. They rouse emotions (a topic we return to in Chapter 8), which induce energy and excitement. Energizing objectives give employees a sense of opportunity, duty, and honor. They help employees to feel part of a larger purpose that has meaning for them and others.

Charisma can take many forms, but leaders have the obligation to create energy and excitement in those they lead. At a minimum, this means expressing pride in employees and the work they are doing.

Focus

As we discussed in Chapter 2, focus is critical to the achievement of any objective. When we talk to executives, we ask, "What is the message you want employees to know?" When the answer is crisp— "We are trying to turn business *A* around by cutting supplier and product costs and to grow business *B* through product innovation"— we have confidence in the objective. When we hear a litany of good ideas, we worry about focus. Simplicity, repetition, and consistency increase focus. Simple messages fit into memorable symbols or icons. Messages repeated consistently ensure focus.

Identify Measures

Sustainable accountability has to link to measures that align with strategy and tie to concrete, specific indicators that can be tracked (see Chapter 7). Incorrect measures hurt the business by misdirecting employee attention to the wrong things just because they are measured. Or they cry wolf so often that they mask real problems when they occur. Leaders have the obligation to create effective measures that focus both individual and organizational attention.

It's useful to think of measures in terms of two dimensions— target and indicator—as outlined in Table 4.2. The target is the unit whose work is being measured, shown here as the individual or collective, and the indicators are what is being measured, which may be behavior (actions) or outcomes (results). This leads to four types of trackable measures.

Table 4.2   Types of Measures and Standards

Indicators	Targets	
	Individual	Collective
Behavior (actions)	**1** Individual behavior (competencies)	**3** Collective behaviors (team processes)
Outcomes (results)	**2** Individual outcomes (management by objectives)	**4** Collective outcomes (unit performance)

Measurement Options

- *Cell 1: Individual behavior measures.* These focus on what people do in a company. Leaders might track how employees demonstrate competencies (e.g., with 360-degree feedback) or how people spend time (e.g., with time sheets that track clients served in a consulting firm). Measures in this cell often apply when outcomes are difficult to define (such as in research and development operations).
- *Cell 2: Individual outcomes measures.* These focus on the results employees deliver. Leaders might create a management-by-objectives measurement system where the specific outcomes for each employee are specified. These types of measures work best where individuals produce results independently (as in sales).
- *Cell 3: Collective behavior measures.* These focus on how teams or organization units work together (e.g., with quarterly team reviews). Leaders can create measures of team effectiveness, and these types of measures are important where teamwork is critical to success.
- *Cell 4: Collective outcomes measures.* These focus on the results of the organization unit. Leaders may define outcomes of a unit in terms of volume, margin, quality, or service. These types of measures emphasize the outcome of the entire unit. Cell 4 is the domain of the balanced scorecard.

We find that organizations with sustainable accountability have measures in all four cells. You can do a quick assessment of your organization's current measurement practices by dividing 100 points across these four types of measures. Allocate the points based on the measurement efforts used now. If the majority of your points fall under the outcomes focus, consider increasing your efforts to make the outcomes repeatable. If the majority of your points fall under the behavior focus, then look at what you are doing to make sure that the behaviors are connected to a clear outcome. What you want is a distribution that encourages behavior that drives outcomes that will increase sustainability.

Ensure Consequences

Sustainable accountability comes when consequences are tied to measures. Consequences may be broadly defined as negative or positive. Negative consequences imply that missing a standard leads to some form of punishment. Negative consequences generally have a short-term impact, driving behavior change because of fear. When those pressures are removed, the original behaviors often come back because every unwilling act of obedience was accompanied by thoughts of what would be done if punishment is not imminent. Positive consequences tend to have a longer-term effect on behavior because it's likelier that behavior repeatedly reinforced by desirable results will become a habit.

At work, negative consequences include taking something away (e.g., salary cuts, dismissal) or removing opportunities (e.g., loss of a promotion or job opportunity). Positive consequences vary by individual, providing more of whatever the individual employee wants from the work itself. People have different needs, making some rewards more valuable than others to a given individual. Some people are more driven by financial rewards and others by opportunities for impact. These individual drives can evolve over a career cycle or as a result of other personal factors. Overall, they have a more lasting impact on accountability than negative consequences do because they focus on the future and what can be, and they encourage learning. Leaders are more likely to drive accountability through positive consequences than negative ones.

Provide Ongoing Feedback

Without feedback, employees won't have sustainable accountability because they won't have the opportunity to reflect, change, and learn. Accountability requires that employees know how they are doing, in clear and unambiguous terms, so that they can modify what they do in the future. Perhaps the greatest flaw in feedback is not giving or soliciting any at all. The loudest feedback leaders give employees is none. When an employee does something wrong and the leader says nothing, the employee hears that what was wrong is right, that leaders don't care, or that leaders don't have the courage to lead. Leaders may wrongly hesitate to share negative news for fear of offense or for lack of courage. Employees may not want to solicit feedback for fear of not being able to respond and with the often false hope that unspoken mistakes may not really have mattered in the first place.

Leaders who want accountability need to step up to the challenge and learn to both give and receive feedback. Like consequences, feedback can and should be both positive and negative. Managers are often pulled toward negative feedback, focusing on employee mistakes and what has gone wrong. Leaders who care about sustainability balance positive feedback, focusing on what employees do well and how to enhance it, with constructive feedback, talking candidly to employees when they need to improve. One leader set an agenda among his team to "focus on what people do, not what they don't." He coached his leadership team to find something positive that an employee was doing, acknowledge it, encourage it, thank the employee for it, and ask the employee what could be done to maintain performance at that level.

Feedback is essentially about follow-up. It is amazing to us the number of leadership improvement efforts that "end" at the end of an event (e.g., coaching session, performance meeting, training program). Follow-up means that leaders who want to improve are accountable not only to themselves, but to someone else. This follow-up may be as simple as a phone call or as complex as weaving behaviors into the HR performance process. It may be done by the trainer or coach, by the leader's leader, or by peers. But, follow-up is essential to sustained change.

By following these four phases of holding others accountable, leaders are more likely to sustain change in themselves as well as others.

Conclusion: Leaders as Responsible Adults

Who, me? Yes, me ... and you!

To ensure accountability in themselves and in others with whom they work, leaders must be responsible adults. We started this chapter with the child's inquiry—"Who, me?"—as a way to introduce accountability as a key factor for sustainability. The four principles we suggest move accountability from child's play to helping leaders to be personally accountable and instill accountability in others. Leaders who take personal responsibility own the changes they advocate. Leaders who go public make a visible commitment to change. Leaders who build a personal brand consistent with their values commit to a new level of performance. Leaders who hold others accountable ensure continuity in their actions and the actions of others. Politicians, educators, parents, and leaders who master these principles build sustainability.

iphone: **RedLaser**
Android: **Barcode Scanner**

Scan this QR code to watch a video about ensuring accountability.

leadershipsustainability.com/qr/accountability

CHAPTER 5

RESOURCES

5

Coaches have to watch for what they don't want to see and listen to what they don't want to hear.

—*John Madden*

Leaders who know why and what they should change are more likely to accomplish their desires when they have the support of those around them. Ultimately, leadership is a team, not an individual activity. Isolated actions are more difficult to sustain because they lack support. Thus the most important resources for leaders to access are human resources, both for themselves and for their organizations. It turns out that when desired behaviors are reinforced by personal coaching and institutionalized in human resources (HR) practices, they are much more likely to be sustained.

Real-World Use of Resources

Here are two executives who have tapped into the power of human resources to ensure leadership that lasts.

Gina Qiao, Senior Vice President for Human Resources, Lenovo

Lenovo is a US$30 billion Fortune 500 personal technology company— and the number one personal computer (PC) makers globally, serving customers in more than 160 countries. Also, Lenovo is the fastest growing PC maker among the top four vendors globally for three straight years. Dedicated to building exceptionally engineered PCs and mobile Internet devices, Lenovo has built its business on product innovation, a highly efficient global supply chain, and strong strategic execution.

Formed by Lenovo Group's acquisition of the former IBM Personal Computing Division, the company develops, manufactures, and markets reliable, high-quality, secure, and easy-to-use technology products and services. Its product lines include the legendary Think-branded commercial PCs and Idea-branded consumer PCs, as well as servers, workstations, and a family of mobile Internet devices, including tablets and smart phones. Lenovo has major research centers in Yamato, Japan; Beijing, Shanghai, and Shenzhen, China; and Raleigh, North Carolina. Now there are approximately 33,000 employees worldwide in Lenovo.

Gina Qiao has been at Lenovo for 22 years. She worked for nine years in marketing and branding, seven years heading human resources, and then three years leading Lenovo's Strategy and Planning Department, where she was responsible for the company's strategic initiatives and implementation. In 2010, Gina led Lenovo's three-year strategic plan and the development of the company's "Protect and Attack" strategy, today viewed as the key driver for Lenovo's market growth and successful business results. She is currently senior vice president for human resources, where she is responsible for Lenovo's HR strategy and its global culture, ensuring that the company has the required organization structures and human resources policies, practices, and programs to execute the company's business strategy. She works globally, with offices in North Carolina and Beijing. She is one of the most respected HR executives in China.

As chief HR officer and member of the Lenovo executive committee, Gina helps Lenovo build the talent and culture to deliver on its strategy. To succeed in this executive role, Gina receives coaching from Yang Yuanqing, Lenovo's CEO, with whom she has worked for many years, from her peers on the executive committee, from her HR employees, and from an external coach. Gina solicits and filters advice from these coaches as she works to be a successful global executive.

Lenovo's Protect and Attack strategy has played a key role in the company's success. Lenovo's strategy also evolves each year. The Protect area is the core businesses, referred to as the "profit pool." By executing the Protect strategy, the company delivers on commitments to its investors and ensures investment in long-term development. The Attack area is the higher-growth space, where the aim is to achieve strong growth and establish a position for long-term development. Lenovo's Protect and Attack success was built on the foundation of its effective business model, innovation leadership, and the "Lenovo Way" culture.

HR supports these strategies by helping to shape the culture and by ensuring talent for growth. Gina helped to manage the complex cultural integration when IBM sold its PC business to Lenovo. This required identifying ways to connect IBM's Western orientation with Lenovo's Eastern work philosophy. Lenovo revised its corporate culture to reflect the globalization. At that time, new values such as "teamwork cross culture" represented the principles of inclusion, respect, and compromise, which Lenovo regarded (and still regards) as guidance for a smooth integration. During the global financial crisis, Lenovo launched a global culture rebuilding project. As a result, Lenovo now believes that its culture, called the Lenovo Way, is what defines the company. This culture captures the company's values, business practices, and day-to-day commitments by reinforcing that at Lenovo people do what they say and own what they do. The Lenovo Way captures culture in the statement highlighting four *P*'s:

- We *plan* before we pledge.
- We *perform* as we promise.
- We *prioritize* the company first.
- We *practice* improving every day.

With the input of her coaches and based on her personal insights, in 2012, Gina introduced a fifth *P—pioneer*—that calls on Lenovo to seek new ideas, take risks, tolerate failures, and encourage innovation. As architect and advocate of the Lenovo culture, Gina has helped to raise the bar on delivering breakthrough innovations, award-winning designs, and strong financial performance.

In addition, Gina reinforces the strategy and culture by designing and delivering HR practices that engage people. Lenovo's people share a common aspiration to be the very best by serving customers, working together as a team, and contributing to the community. Gina believes that Lenovo's talent strength lies in diversity, in its ability to capture the best of the East and West. HR practices fully support its people and sustain their culture. The five *P*'s are a part of a Lenovo leader's competency model; they are appraised and taken into account for rewards; they are communicated broadly; they are part of the employee voice survey; and they have an impact on career decisions.

By being an architect and advocate of the culture, talent, and HR systems, Gina helps to make sure that Lenovo has the resources to focus, sustain, and accomplish its strategic agenda.

Agung Adiprasetyo, CEO, Kompas Gramedia

The Indonesian company Kompas Gramedia started in 1963 by publishing *Intisari* magazine. P. K. Oyong and Jakob Oetama, cofounders of Kompas Gramedia, both come from a teaching background, which reinforces the company vision to contribute by enlightening people. This enlightenment is supported by two values. First, the company cares about human value. Second, the company values integrity. The founders believe that the values of caring and integrity will help everybody in the company to feel that the company belongs to them, thus leading to growth.

Kompas Gramedia grew as Media Company, with the *Kompas* newspaper published in June 1965. Today, Kompas Gramedia has become the largest media company in Indonesia, managing 24 newspapers, 90 magazine titles, 15 radio stations, 11 television stations, and other ventures with web publishing, a printing plant and bookstore, and book publishing. Besides its core media operations, it also has expanded into the hotel business, toll roads, and the tissue paper business. This philosophy of expanding business broadens the company's chance to absorb personnel in Indonesia and help the government decrease unemployment.

Agung Adiprasetyo has worked with Kompas Gramedia for 29 years. He started as finance staff for one year, moved to the hotel market, then entered the media market. He held increasingly responsible positions, becoming CEO in 2006. He faces three challenges in that office. First, the media industry platform has changed from print to digital and electronic media. Second, the demographic profile in Indonesia has changed; 65 percent of the population is younger than 35 and is highly digitally savvy, whereas 40 percent of the employees at Kompas Gramedia are over 45 years old and find it a challenge to continue to match the expectations of younger users. Third, in 2011, the surviving founder, Jakob Oetama, turned 80 years old. He is a charismatic and legendary leader, but it is critical to prepare his successor. All three challenges must be dealt with in an increasingly competitive environment.

Because of these challenges, Agung and his team have evolved the two foundational values into what they call the "five *C*'s": care, credible, competence, competitive, and customer delight. They believe that renewing these core values will make Kompas Gramedia more relevant within the Indonesia community. With these five new values, Agung shifted his priority to change the way the company is run. He wants to maintain the growth of the company because growth increases employee spirit. To sustain company growth, he believes in three success factors: ideas, execution or implementation, and teamwork. He has worked to embed these success factors throughout the company.

Succeeding through ideas means finding and nurturing people who are very creative, innovative, and conceptual. Teamwork encourages discussion but sometimes keeps leaders from making decisions, and it can make decisions take a long time to implement.

To succeed through talented people, teamwork, and execution, Agung worked to update his management systems. He made sure that leaders and all employees of Kompas Gramedia had a balanced scorecard with clear key performance indicators (KPIs). These KPIs made sure that employees always knew who was responsible for execution and implementation. Then, with information support, it was possible to coordinate the actions of everybody in the company. This performance management system overcame an Indonesian cultural reluctance to set standards, give objective marks for performance, and reprimand, if required.

With this performance management system in place, Agung and his team are more able to sustain their growth goals because they sort the performance of every business every three months. They are able to determine which companies make a good financial contribution and sustain growth and which have less of a contribution and lower growth. They even liquidate some businesses after several years of bad performance.

As a leader, Agung believes in giving time to everybody who works in his subsidiaries. He wants to appreciate the good work they do, but on the other side, when the subsidiaries are not meeting performance standards, he has to make tough and difficult decisions. The company's performance management process gives him a proper way to evaluate performance so that his subsidiaries do the work they are expected to do.

Coordinating Effort

Gina and Agung recognize that coordinated actions sustain more value than isolated individual actions. This discipline of resources applies across the whole range of human experience. In almost every team sport, for example, the leading scorer (top individual performer) is rarely on the team that wins the championship. In the National Basketball Association (NBA), about 15 percent of the time the team with the top scorer wins the NBA championship. When Michael Jordan led the league in scoring while his team missed the NBA championship (four times!), he averaged 34.55 points per game. In the six years that he led the league in scoring and his team won the championship, he averaged 30.5 points per game. Even the best player ever to play the game won more championships when he scored less and when he had a stronger team. In soccer, the winner of the Golden Boot (the player scoring the most goals) is on the team that wins the World Cup only 23 percent of the time. In hockey, the leading scorer is on the team that wins the Stanley Cup 23 percent of the time. Teamwork magnifies individual action.

In politics, the European Union helps individual countries become stronger together. The United Arab Emirates brings countries in its region together, too; for example, Abu Dhabi recently helped Dubai through the real estate crisis. In these political settings, individual provinces or states come together to forge a stronger federal union. For enterprises, isolated establishments pool resources to enable them to source materials, operate efficiently, and serve customers. Walmart's enormous success has come because of its ability to move beyond single stores into an integrated domestic and global brand. Small mom-and-pop stores cannot compete.

Within organizations, unified action continues to outpace individual effort, but the effect is strongest when the organization is set up to promote collective work. Coaching and leveraging human resources are critical ways to sustain desired leadership change. Our experience shows that the transfer of learning from a training program or 360-degree feedback process increases dramatically when supported by coaching. We have found that when a company invests money in a multiday leadership training program, about 20 to 30 percent of what is learned is applied. This impact doubles with personal coaching. At Mobily, a Saudi-based telecommunications company, we have taught three three-day modules over a 12-month period. Before, during, and between each module, participants received expert coaching. These personal coaching sessions start with participants receiving feedback on their style and their performance. The output of the initial coaching is to develop an individual development plan that clarifies personal improvement goals. The training sessions offer theory, research, cases, and tools for improvement, and the follow-up coaching between modules tailors the application to each participant. The 20 percent increased cost of the program with coaching doubles the level of improvement in application of the ideas (from 30 to 60 percent), which means that there is a 5:1 return on coaching.

In this chapter we offer specific insights about how leaders can use coaches to find personal support and how they can make sure that the HR infrastructure reinforces these desired changes. Because most leaders are familiar with the basics of coaching, we move straight to a definition of the different types of coaches and discuss how to best use a coach for yourself and for others on your team.

Coaching

Coaching sustains change because it personalizes and reinforces a leader's intent for the future. As with many professions, business coaching began slowly and often received mixed results. In the last 20 years, as leadership coaching has mushroomed, the range of coaching expectations and services has exploded, for both good and ill. To use coaching to sustain change, leaders should answer four questions:

- What outcomes should I expect from coaching?
- Who can I work with as my coach?
- What should I do to receive good coaching?
- What skills should I expect from my coach?

Outcomes to Expect

One of our shortest and most memorable coaching experiences was with a high-potential family member of an executive team. We were honored to be invited to coach him as he prepared for his likely succession to run the large family business. When we began our conversation, we asked him why he wanted to be coached and what he wanted out of the experience. He seemed surprised by the question and replied in an off-hand manner with something like, "I just need to tell the board that I am being coached by someone reputable so that I can be seen as ready to move into my next leadership role." When we probed what he wanted in terms of business or personal outcomes, he brushed us aside, saying, "You tell me." It was not a long engagement. He was not ready to be coached and was totally unaware of the outcomes of coaching. He wanted a coach because he needed to check it off on his development plan for his next promotion.

Individuals and companies engage in coaching for a host of reasons, often disjointed, as set out in Figure 5.1. Each of these outcomes may make sense for the individual, but without an overarching framework, coaching will not be sustainable.

To lead to sustainable change, coaching needs to be based on a more rigorous typology of outcomes. In the spirit of simplicity advocated in Chapter 2, we offer a typology of coaching outcomes based on two dimensions: First, does the coaching focus primarily on changing behaviors or on delivering results? And second, does the coaching focus more on the individual or the organization? With these two dimensions in mind, the coaching outcomes sketched in Figure 5.1 can be categorized as shown in Figure 5.2.

Figure 5.1   *Potential coaching outcomes.*

Figure 5.2   *A typology of coaching outcomes.*

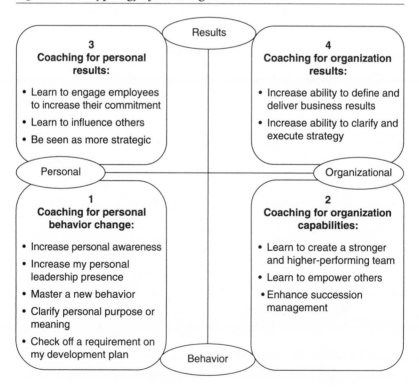

1. *Coaching for personal behavior change.* Leaders sustain personal behavior change when they identify specific behaviors that can and should be changed; coaches provide feedback and advice about how to make those new behaviors consistently happen.
2. *Coaching to build organization capabilities.* Leaders sustain change when their coaches help them to frame and build the right organization capabilities or culture to institutionalize their personal changes.
3. *Coaching for personal results.* Leaders sustain change when their coaches help them to see the valued outcomes or personal results that come from the change.
4. *Coaching for organization results.* Leaders sustain change when coaches help them to link their actions to long-term organization results.

When leaders work with coaches to be clear on their desired outcome, the changes they desire are more likely to be sustained because the role of the coach can be defined and tracked. Coaching is a resource to sustain change.

Choice of Coach

We have identified five coaching archetypes. Each archetype represents an individual a leader can turn to for coaching that sustains change.

- *Self-coaching.* Leaders coach themselves by being self-aware of their behaviors and desired performance.
- *Peer coaching (internal).* Leaders find allies or friends inside their organizations who can advise and guide them.
- *Peer coaching (external).* Leaders join networks of like-minded professionals outside their organizations for mutual help.

- *Boss coaching.* A leader's direct supervisor coaches behavior and guides changes in results.
- *Expert coaching.* A leader hires a professional coach who has credentials and experience to inform behavior and improve results.

We find this typology enormously helpful when we advise leaders on how to sustain changes by selecting the type of coach that works best for them. Each coaching archetype has strengths and weaknesses when it comes to accomplishing one of the four outcomes of coaching. These coaching types are not mutually exclusive; they can work in tandem to achieve desired outcomes.

Self-Coaching

In some ways, we know ourselves better than anyone else and can employ the most effective form of incentive—internal motivation. Self-coaching occurs when we self-monitor and recognize how our intentions are not aligned with our actions. At some level, self-coaching is the most ideal and efficient. When leaders recognize their own predispositions and act on them, they are more likely to make change stick. Dave knows, for example, that he is predisposed to being an introvert. Therefore, when he teaches or gives talks, he knows that he has to overcome this tendency and engage the group in conversation. Norm knows that he tends to wander when he teaches, so he has to be very disciplined at preparing and following an agenda to keep focused.

Leaders who self-coach need to remain aware of their personal predispositions and how they come across to others. They need to see how others are responding to them. Self-coaching takes time. Leaders need to carve out space to reflect on what worked and what did not work. Ego should not be invested in what they have done or who they are, and they need to be willing to publicly acknowledge that they are changing. Leaders should solicit and then listen to feedback without being defensive and employ self-discipline to change.

One leader we worked with had received some feedback that his tendency to let his frustrations out was affecting the morale of his employees. Deciding to work on the issue, he examined the triggers that set him off and went public with his employees to discuss his triggers. He asked for their help as he worked to keep his frustrations in check. He now reports a much happier workplace environment and less personal stress on everyone.

Self-monitoring has its drawbacks, too. Another executive we coached wanted to make sure that his team made the best possible decisions. He often intervened in team decision making—advocating his recommended decision. His intent was to improve decisions, and he felt that he was succeeding. Unfortunately for him, his team members saw him as intrusive, micromanaging, and autocratic, so they withdrew and became passive observers. It turns out that there's truth in the saying that a lawyer who represents himself has a fool for a client. Doctors who self-medicate risk losing their licenses. And it's easy to be over-confident about progress in self-coaching, accepting the intentions and glossing over the actions. As noted earlier, this is a perpetual human failing; Marshall Goldsmith reports that 80 percent of the people he's studied rate themselves in the top 20 percent of performance—a clear sign that many are judging their intentions and not their outcomes.

Peer Coaching (Internal)

Leaders who use peer coaching often have a friend at work who cares for them. As a friend, this peer observes the behaviors and results of the leader yet knows the intentions. In informal and casual settings, the peer coach can help the leader to change behaviors and deliver better results. Leaders who take the personal risk of asking their work allies how they are doing will quickly learn whether a friend can also be a coach. Friends who do not give honest feedback—even when asked— may stay friends, but they are not peer coaches. Great leaders seek out insightful peers who are willing to be coaches. One leader intentionally sought out allies on her team and throughout the organization who would privately let her know how she was doing. These allies were peer coaches and an invaluable source of insight on her leadership style.

Peer coaches need not always be in the same line of business within an organization. We've seen much success when leaders from different business units of the same firm get together on a regular basis to discuss areas they're working to improve and issues with which they're grappling. The same types of issues arise around the organization, and hearing a different perspective on possible solutions and proven practices can be instructive.

Relying only on peers has limitations; peers may not see the whole picture, and they may lack a deep understanding of the leader's motives and expectations. Friends acting as peer coaches also may be less objective than they could be—not wanting to put the friendship under the stress that frank observations might create.

Peer Coaching (External)

Social networking has changed how strangers connect with each other. For example, a fascinating movement exists today in which older adults who want to stay in their own homes join a village network organization that connects them to others in similar circumstances. About a hundred of these villages exist in the United States, and their numbers are growing rapidly; independent people pay a fee to join the village and then serve each other. Heretofore strangers connect with each other in ways such as these[1]:

- Ferni, 53, an options trader, provides computer coaching to Susan, 73, a retired family nurse.
- Susan helps Carole, 68, a retired college administrator, organize her files in her new apartment.
- And so on. It generally works out that everyone in such a group can do something that someone else needs and needs something that someone else can happily do.

If social networking helps retired individuals learn and grow, it can also help leaders. We suggest four types of networks where people come together with an agenda to improve. In each of these networks, leaders can connect with those outside their organizations to gain insight and become better:

Relationship networks. The people we go to when we want to have fun. The Gallup organization has argued that everyone needs to have a best friend at work. We would argue that it is even more important for leaders to have a best friend (outside the family) *not* at work and who does not have a stake in the work setting.

Knowledge networks. The people we go to when we need information. Leaders can be encouraged to join professional associations, to create cohort groups of peers, and to attend conferences to meet and associate with peers who have ideas to solve problems.

Trust networks. The people we go to with personal or confidential information. Leaders may find trusted advisors in neighborhoods, religious associations, social groups, long-time friends, or extended family to whom they turn for personal questions and insights.

Purpose networks. The people we go to when we need to accomplish a task. Leaders may get insights from consultants, advisors, former faculty, or other experts about projects they need to accomplish.

Depending on the network, these peers outside work offer insights on sustaining both behavior and results. All networks must be nurtured or they fade.

Boss Coaching

In one company, a senior executive quashed the coaching budget because she felt that a leader's immediate boss was the most important source for coaching, and she did not want anything to detract from that relationship. In many ways, she was right. Leaders who coach and communicate rather than command and control have enormous opportunities for impact. In other ways, she was wrong. People often need to be able to explore a range of issues in coaching— some of which may include their relationship with their boss, their future with the company, and other personal issues unlikely to be discussed when the boss is the coach.

Bosses who coach need to develop not only a mind-set but a skill set. Instead of demanding results or providing solutions, they learn to ask thoughtful questions and listen to understand. Because all bosses can and should be coaches, we identify key questions bosses can master to improve their coaching skills (Table 5.1).

Table 5.1   Coaching Questions for Bosses

Principles of Coaching	Coaching Questions Bosses Should Be Asking
Build relationship of trust	How can I be helpful? What would you like from this conversation? Help me understand ...
Describe current performance	What are the results you are after? How well do you think you have done? Why? What led you to this current result? What do you do that helps or hinders reaching your goal?
Articulate desired results	What would you like to accomplish? How do you feel about the outcome you are after? How will you know when you have succeeded?
Build an action plan for change	What actions could you take to reach your goal? What are the pros and cons of each? What are the first steps you need to take? What can I do to help you be successful? How will you learn from things that don't go well? Who will you be accountable to for progress?

Bosses who can ask questions rather than jump to answers, who seek to understand before giving direction, and who work to build trust before taking action can become excellent coaches. Leaders wanting to improve should be able to rely on their boss not only for performance reviews but also for career counseling, where the boss can point the leader in a positive direction.

However, bosses as coaches also have limitations. The Lominger group found that of the 67 key skills for business leaders, coaching is toward the bottom. Many bosses rise to their positions of influence not by coaching but by doing. They are competent, but they are not able to multiply that competence in others—a lack that is a major source of derailment as people reach the higher levels to which they have aspired.

Expert Coaching

Expert coaching may take a variety of forms. A company can hire trained coaches as permanent employees to work with other employees across departments or functions, or it can call on outside consultants— psychologists or specialists in personal or organizational development. The choice of an individual coach is always a complex decision. Coaching certifications, like all certifications, ensure that the coach has basic knowledge, not that the coach will be successful in a specific relationship or even in general. This is the same situation other professions face; a licensed attorney, architect, or psychologist has certified that he or she knows the basics of the profession, but the license does not mean such a person can practice well.

Expert coaches can help leaders to sustain changes in both behavior and results. They may explore candid (and at times brutal) information about the leader's behavior and performance. They may make suggestions about how to improve and challenge the status quo. They also may help the leader to create a personal leadership brand by combining behavior and results into a leadership identity. One senior leader we coached told us, "When you come into my office, I am your primary agenda. Everyone else who sees me has an agenda of what they want to get from me, either explicitly or implicitly. Your agenda is giving to me." That made the sessions especially enjoyable.

Expert coaches help leaders when their insights turn into effective actions. However, expert coaches also have limitations. They do not live inside the organization and see the day-to-day operations. They may be used as sounding boards without real accountability for action. As expert coaches, we have found it most useful if we meet with the leader's HR head before and after the coaching session. The HR head can alert the expert coach to current political issues in the organization and to challenges the leader is facing with others before the coaching session. After the session, while maintaining confidentiality, the leader's HR head is in a position to ensure that the follow-up is sustained.

Enabling Good Coaching

Two broad issues are relevant to using coaching as a source of sustainability. First, consider who can and should be most open to coaching as a vehicle for sustainability. We have found that coaching can be used to help

- Business leaders facing new and unforeseen business challenges that require new behaviors
- Leaders throughout the company who have a behavior or style that keeps them from accomplishing what they desire (such as lack of self-awareness or an inability to influence upward)
- Leaders who have had little exposure to or experience outside their home organizations
- Professionals who need to add emotional and social skills to their technical expertise to succeed in their careers
- High-potential employees who need to refine skills to prepare for future career opportunities

Coaching for sustainability may be adapted to each of these target groups and offer the outcomes summarized earlier.

Second, consider whether the individual being coached is serious about long-term change. Every good coach has walked away from an engagement because the commitment of the individual was not adequate for the change required. Some ideas and behaviors that indicate a likelihood of sustaining change include

- Openness to change
- Willingness to experiment with ideas
- Ability to reflect on and acknowledge mistakes
- Willingness to listen to what others say with a sense of inquisitiveness and humility
- Openness to learning
- A focus on the future (feed forward) rather than the past (feedback)
- Ability to adapt a style to the requirements of the situation
- A sense a personal mission and passion

Not all individuals will ever be fully prepared for coaching, but they should be aware that it is more than casual conversation and dialogue; it is serious and hard work to reflect, define behaviors, identify required behavior changes, and sustain those changes. It requires a candor and openness that many hard-shelled executives don't want to admit or face.

Expectations of a Coach

A coach who helps an individual sustain change is able to manage both content and process. *Content* refers to the coach's point of view about what it means to be an effective leader who delivers sustainable results. This point of view is tied to the situation of the organization's business context, strategy, and team and to the gender and experience of the individual being coached, but the coach needs to have a mental model that goes beyond those factors. If you are choosing among expert coaches, ask about the candidates' view of what makes an effective leader. If the response is not crisp, the coach is unlikely to be effective.

Process refers to the engagement between the coach and client. Here are some guidelines coaches can follow to make sure that their coaching can be used for sustainable leadership behaviors:

- Focus on the future, not the past.
- Build a trusting relationship in which the individual knows that you care about him or her as a person.
- Recognize, discover, and build on the passion, meaning, and desires of the individual.
- Listen for understanding.
- Ask probing questions that bring deeper issues to the surface.
- Respect and build on the strengths of the individual, but do not hesitate to label and address the weaknesses.
- Be candid without being punishing.
- Use data from many sources (e.g., 360-degree feedback or observation) to help the individual recognize unintended consequences.
- Find the right physical setting in which to coach.
- Use time wisely.
- Build sustainability into the coaching engagement by follow-up and accountability.
- Be very sensitive to unique qualities (e.g., gender, religious orientation, global experience, or personal history) of the individual and be open to talk about these sensitive areas.

When leaders use coaches to help sustain their behaviors, their chosen behaviors will be more likely to endure over time.

Institutionalizing Change Through HR Practices

Organization systems enable sustainable personal change because they signal, reinforce, and encourage it. A leader who wants to change but finds that the change is not supported by organization policies is torn between the personal goal and the organization policy. When policies and practices do support personal change, such change is more likely to happen.

Many organization policies that sustain change are found in HR practices. We have chosen to talk about the work of HR as a set of HR practices because a practice is something that is continually being learned (we practice a musical instrument or a sport). A practice is also an activity within a profession (the practice of law). We have summarized HR practices into four flows, each of which can be used to sustain change.

- *Flow of people.* What happens to the organization's key asset—its people—including how people move in, through, up, and out of the organization.
- *Flow of performance management.* What links people to work—the standards and measures, financial and nonfinancial rewards, and feedback that reflect stakeholder interests.
- *Flow of information.* What links people to knowledge—what they need to know to do their work and how they get the requisite information. Information can flow up, down, or laterally. It can flow from the outside in or from the inside out.
- *Flow of work.* What links tasks to people—who does the work, how the work is done, where the work is done, and how the work is supported through business and operating processes to combine individual efforts into organizational outputs.

When these HR practices are used to reinforce new leadership behaviors, leaders are more likely to sustain them over time. The simple principle is to make sure that HR practices reinforce the desired behaviors.

Flow of People

An individual leader who wants to sustain a personal change will be encouraged and validated when multiple HR practices reinforce that change. Whether a leader is trying to be more innovative and creative, more disciplined and efficient, or more collaborative, these behaviors should show up in the flow of talent: hiring, orienting, training, career planning and promotion, and outplacement.

Who a company hires sends signals about what behaviors are most in demand. Google's extensive screening process validates the importance of innovation in its operations. A leader who wants to be more innovative will be encouraged when innovative behaviors are woven into the hiring decision. Leaders attempting to sustain change can help to set criteria for the types of individuals they want to hire.

How a company develops its employees also reinforces the desired behaviors. When the training initiatives offer content that is related to strategy, the principles being imparted in the training are more likely to be implemented. In recent years, action learning has been replaced with learning solutions in which the purpose is less about taking action and more about using training as a setting to learn new ways to solve problems. In many cases, a leader may learn about a needed change through a 360-degree feedback process, performance review, or other mechanism and then select a training course or development experience to provide the skills and tools to inform the desired change.

In recent years, most have accepted that leadership improvement comes more from experience than formal training. While we agree, we are worried that the "lessons from experience" movement focuses more on "experience" than on "lessons." Just having a new experience does not ensure improvement. Leaders need to learn to access "lessons" from their experiences by rigorous and thoughtful reflection from questions such as: What worked? What did not work? Why? What are the principles that I can adapt from this experience? What would I tell someone that I learned? What would I do differently? How can I ensure that I will transfer the insights from this experience to another setting? When can I specifically apply those insights next? These questions ensure that experiences cumulate in lessons learned.

Who is promoted and how careers are managed go a long way to sustain change—or undercut it. For example, one leader we coached wanted to improve by engaging his employees in decision making. When he returned to his work setting, he did listen better and encourage participation, but the standards for his performance did not change, so his improvement did not show up in his performance review. And even more difficult for him, when he was one of the two finalists for a promotion, his new ability to engage employees was not considered, and he was passed over. When he observed that leaders who did not demonstrate the newly found skills were more likely to be promoted, he realized that his behavior changes were not valued by others. In career discussions, leaders who share their desired improvements should learn the extent to which those improvements will increase their ability to reach their career goals.

Ultimately, one of the loudest statements about talent comes from which people are asked to leave the company. People always observe and interpret terminations and attempt to discover or deduce the reasons. When leaders who seek to improve are asked to leave, others seeking to sustain change are discouraged. When the ones asked to leave are those who do not demonstrate the skills the company has stated it values, others recognize that their desired changes are relevant and appreciated.

Integrating personal leadership changes into talent flow practices requires that the leader wanting to change recognize how talent management practices encourage or discourage the desired behavior changes. The leader wanting to change can also engage with an HR professional to candidly assess the extent to which desired changes may be consistent with current practices. Hopefully, the HR professional can make sure that those practices reinforce rather than hinder the change.

Flow of Performance Management

Without doubt, incentives change behavior. People do what they are rewarded for. Leaders get what they reward but not always what they expect. Without clear standards, measured against expected results and linked with the rewards people want, employee behavior can seem very strange.[2] On the other hand, when standards and incentives align with company goals, the goals generally come within reach. For example, 3M makes innovation a goal, and it ties meaningful financial and nonfinancial rewards to a *vitality index*—the percentage of revenue from products introduced in the last three years. The clarity of this index encourages experimentation, risk-taking, and sharing of ideas.

Leaders who want to sustain change need to be publicly recognized and privately rewarded for the changes they are making. These changes should be woven into the performance discussion so that they are clearly defined, made operational, and agreed to. When leaders meet (or miss) their desired behaviors, positive or negative consequences should follow. We see this happening in some places—and not happening in others.

A leader received feedback, coaching, and encouragement to spend more time working in teams than alone. After considering and honestly filtering these recommendations, she took them to heart and prepared a list of behaviors she should do to encourage teamwork. She started to share decisions with her team; she did team-building sessions; she worked on team relationships; and she encouraged her team members to respond more openly to her. While she was building this performance and morale within her team, she felt that she was improving as a leader. When her annual performance review was held, though, her boss did not recognize or acknowledge her efforts to build teamwork. She was judged on much the same criteria as the preceding year even though she had worked hard to improve. As we reflected on this outcome, she realized that she had not been clear enough with her boss or the HR professional about her efforts to improve teamwork. While her team members saw progress, she was not able to document it, nor was she able to point out its effects in her results. If she was not able or willing to have a frank discussion with her boss about her desired team-related behaviors, could not find ways to measure and track performance, and could not weave her progress into her performance review, she would not be likely to sustain the effort.

Another leader we worked with was very gifted at encouraging new behaviors of those on her team. After training sessions, performance reviews, or 360-degree feedback sessions, she would ask each employee to share one or two behaviors they were working to improve. Then, over the year, when she saw an employee consistently demonstrating the new behavior, she would publicly acknowledge it. This might be highlighting the employee's new behavior in a talk, thanking the employee in both private and public, or having the employee tell others about experience with the new behavior. These informal reinforcements complemented the formal financial incentives, and the leader was able to create a learning culture in which employees were able to sustain their desired changes.

Flow of Information

Information is the stuff of which organizations are made, by which they function, and through which they prosper or fail.[3] Information permits a company to identify and meet the demands of competitive markets, creates company value in the eyes of customers and shareholders, and enables a company to function within the ethical parameters of its communities. Through information, organizations share goals, craft strategies, make decisions, and integrate behaviors. Information enables innovation to proceed, change to occur, service and quality to improve, costs to stay under control, and productivity to increase. It determines who has influence over which issues and who does not, giving meaning and direction to work and purpose to the lives of managers and employees alike.

In addition, information signals to employees what is important and should be done and what is not important and should be avoided. When leaders' personal behavior changes can be woven into formal and informal communications, they are more likely to be sustained.

Formal communications include social media, newsletters, websites, company meetings, and executive speeches. Leaders who have access to these forums can share their personal experiences at defining and sustaining change. As we noted in Chapter 3, when leaders go public with their desired changes, the resulting public pressure makes them more likely to sustain the new behavior. For example, a leadership team allocated about 10 to 20 percent of investor call time to talking about the new and desired leadership behaviors in their company. By sharing expectations with investors, the leaders put pressure on themselves to track and document the changes they were promising. By the nature of their roles and responsibilities, leaders make public statements about what matters most to them. When these statements include leadership behaviors, the changes are more likely to occur.

Informally, leaders constantly interact with others. Through those interactions, they signal what matters most to them. Leaders often demonstrate their new desired behaviors in their private, not public moments. We have worked with leaders who have very different public and private personas. In public, they are engaging, encouraging, and upbeat, but in private, they are demanding, demeaning, and demoralizing. In a world of increased transparency, these leaders' personal behaviors will become increasingly public. When leaders attend as much to their private and informal interactions as to their public ones, or more, they are more likely to sustain new behaviors.

A leader we worked with wanted to become more charitable and generous with both time and resources. Rather than go public with these aspirations, she started adapting private behaviors. She wrote thank-you notes to employees who were successful; she walked to employee offices to share information rather than asking employees to come to her; and she started socializing a little more with employees (e.g., taking someone to lunch, asking about the employee's family). At first, no one really noticed because these changes were not advertised, but after about three or four months of consistently working on it, she began to recognize a difference. As we worked with her, we learned from her employees that they began to notice and share their experiences. An employee would share that he got a note from her, then another employee would say that he had also, and another would share that she sent his son a birthday gift. As these informal stories mounted, the leader began to shift her identity, and the new behaviors became more ingrained and natural.

Formal or informal information sharing requires a personal risk that comes from transparency. Often leaders don't want to formally or informally acknowledge what they want to change for fear that it will diminish them in the eyes of others. We have found that this is a serious cognitive distortion; the opposite is what is true. Most observers of leaders know the behaviors that need to be changed. When leaders privately or publicly acknowledge this, others are impressed and willing to support the leader in sustaining the change. Change happens when the leader does it; it is sustained when peers and others come to expect it.

Flow of Work

How work is organized and administered ultimately transforms ideas and raw materials into products and services. Organizations adopt cultures, roles, and routines that sustain leaders' behaviors and actions. These cultures often outlive the individuals who pass through them. The Walmart culture of cost consciousness is likely to outlive any individual leader; the Apple culture of innovation will endure beyond the loss of Steve Jobs' genius. When leaders can make their personal behaviors consistent with the organization's culture, they are likely to be sustained. It is not just the leader acting in isolation but the leader reflecting and supporting a desired culture that has a truly lasting effect. We believe that an organization's culture moves from isolated events (e.g., a leader's talk, a compensation plan, a training program) to integrated patterns (e.g., how employees think and act in their organization) to an identity of how the organization is known by its external stakeholders, or from the outside in.

We have worked with many companies to create sustainable cultures by focusing them from the outside in. This means that the culture represents the identity of the organization in the minds of key stakeholders outside the organization (e.g., customers or investors). When these external expectations are clear, they create a firm brand that positions the organization in the marketplace. But these external expectations are not sustainable until they turn into leadership behaviors (what we have called a *leadership brand*). When leadership behaviors match external expectations, they are much more sustainable because they deliver tangible value to customers and investors.

Individual leaders who want to sustain their desired behavior changes do so more effectively when they have a line of sight between their new actions and the expectations of external stakeholders. When a leader can show that the new ability to experiment with ideas and take risks will be consistent with key customer expectations of innovation, these new behaviors are more likely to be sustained. This is why we advocate doing 720-degree reviews and not just 360-degree reviews for many leaders. The 360-degree process collects information from individuals inside the organization; the 720-degree process collects information from outside as well. When leaders' desired behaviors match firm brand, their actions are not just personal whims—they offer definitive value added.

Culture and related leader behaviors are often sustained through organization structure and administrative routines. *Organization structure* refers to the roles, rules, and responsibilities of the leader. When new behaviors are clearly related to a leader's role and responsibilities, they are more likely to be of personal value to the leader because they help the leader on the job. A leader we coached was promoted from a group of peers, becoming the vice president of her division. In this role, she realized that she had increased responsibility for shaping the strategy of her group. She attended a strategic planning workshop to learn the frameworks and logic of strategy; she observed good strategists in her company to learn what they do; and she received coaching to shift her behavior to that of a strategist. As she engaged in new strategic behaviors (e.g., anticipating the future, understanding social trends, allocating scarce resources against strategic priorities), she recognized that these new behaviors were critical to her new role. The behaviors endured because they enabled her to fulfill her duties.

Administrative routines are also important to sustain leader behaviors. As noted earlier, many of the routines in a company are unwritten rules that leaders need to recognize and master to succeed. In one company, a leader was struggling with being accepted because he constantly violated the unwritten rules that were core to the company. When we coached him, we helped him to observe his work environment so that he could recognize the unwritten rules (e.g., when and how to push back, what information to share, and how fast to make decisions). As he began to weave these unwritten rules into his personal behaviors, he was more able to sustain his change because it fit the routines of the company. In addition, there were formal administrative routines or policies that leaders needed to recognize to sustain their change. These policies were often around the flow of work: vacation days and times, work hours, working locations, attire at work, use of computers, and so on. When the leader was able to recognize these administrative policies, he was more able to make sure that his personal behaviors were consistent with them.

Conclusion: Leaders as Teammates

We have talked about coaching and infrastructure resources to help leaders sustain their desired personal changes. Leaders acting alone, even with great desire and good intentions, are unlikely to sustain their desired changes. When they receive support from all types of coaches who are clear about outcomes and processes, and when their desired behaviors are woven into the flow of people, performance, information, and work, they will find themselves able to sustain change.

iphone: **RedLaser**
Android: **Barcode Scanner**

Scan this QR code to watch a video about leveraging the right resources.

leadershipsustainability.com/qr/resources

CHAPTER 6

TRACKING

6

Measure twice, cut once.

—English proverb

You really do get what you inspect and not what you expect. And people really do what they are rewarded for, so it is pointless to hope for one thing while rewarding another. These axioms apply to sustaining both personal and organizational change.

Real-World Tracking

Here are two examples of finding ways to promote goals by choosing the right details to monitor.

Dixon Thayer, CEO, HealthNext

Dixon Thayer, a serial entrepreneur, is currently CEO of HealthNext— an emerging leader in establishing workforce wellness as a measurable competitive advantage. Thayer sees huge opportunities for improving the health-care industry by bringing a strong business eye to its practices. Since employer health-care costs in America continue to grow two to four times faster than general inflation, success here represents a huge competitive advantage, and Thayer believes that measuring improvement is a key to success. He maintains that a few benchmark organizations are "bending the curve of productivity and cost" without reducing benefits or shifting costs to their employees.

Dixon is a strong believer in two guiding principles that can drive behavior change of leaders:

- What gets measured gets improved.
- Three core questions drive continuous improvement:
  o How are we doing?
  o How can we make it better?
  o What if?

Dixon argues that most approaches to measuring health-care costs focus on factors that leaders can't control—and that it's critical to measure what leaders can control to drive real change. He describes a virtuous cycle starting with actions driving awareness,

Which, in turn, drives engagement
Which, in turn, drives behavior change
Which, in turn, drives biometric improvement
Which, in turn, drives outcomes
Which, in turn, drives return on investment (ROI)

For this virtuous cycle to work, measurement and reporting must be structured to identify value and reward alignment and participation at each stage rather than waiting years for indirect actuarial results. Some sample metrics include

- The number and degree of programs implemented (measuring actions)
- The percentage of the target population participating in specific programs (engagement)

- Key performance indicators (KPIs) based on type and change in population biometrics (improvements)
- Benchmarking to others to identify sources of learning (enduring continuous improvement)
- Estimating the value of a particular initiative, where possible (ROI)

Approaching tracking in this way results in a straightforward dashboard that is simple to understand and easy to respond to with action designed to improve costs and employee behaviors. The one Dixon set up tracks each of the three core questions (How are we doing? How can we make it better? What if?) against HealthNEXT's various locations using color-coding to flag issues that are critical to fix now (red), issues that may become problems in the near future (yellow), and issues that are in good shape (green).

iphone: **RedLaser**
Android: **Barcode Scanner**

Scan this QR code to watch a case study about HealthNEXT by CEO Dixon Thayer.

leadershipsustainability.com/qr/tracking

Your Authors on Safari

Dave and Norm have had the opportunity to do African safaris connected to work opportunities in Johannesburg. Within a relatively short distance of the city, it's possible to visit Kruger National Park or even go further to Chobe National Park in Botswana. Safari companies offer multiple options around degree of comfort. Both of us spent a little extra money and experienced a relatively luxurious version of camping: We stayed in a lodge during the heat of the day when the animals were less active and rode in an open truck with extended seats to see the animals in the early morning and at dusk, when they tended to be out and about.

The intent of any safari goer is to see the "big five" animals—lions, leopards, elephants, cape buffaloes, and rhinos. On one trip, our tracker was a native African named Abraham. Abraham grew up in a village not far from the park. He had been a tracker for 30 years and had an amazing gift for finding the desired animals in the right place at the right time. At critical points, he would jump out of the truck and examine the dirt beside the trail, which sometimes was a paved road and other times a narrow path. We were constantly amazed at his ability to squat and stare at the dirt and then direct us to see the animals we came to see. Where we simply saw dirt, he saw unique animal tracks. He could not only discern the kind of animal but also often whether the tracks were from a male or a female, how many animals there were, what direction they were moving, how fast they were moving, when they had last eaten, and how recently they had been there.

Most of us don't track wild animals, but we can learn from Abraham the importance of tracking to ensure sustainability. The only way to know if we are successful is to track and measure desired changes. Our safari experience would have been very different if we were not concerned about seeing certain kinds of animals. Knowing which animals we wanted to see and then looking for them and tracking our progress made the safari more interesting and rewarding.

Tracking in the Workplace

To sustain organizational change, it is necessary to track organization processes and their outcomes and see if they lead to desired outcomes. In personal and organization settings, tracking data has moved from information (e.g., data bases that report stand-alone metrics) to analysis (e.g., summaries and trends) to insight and prediction (e.g., discovery of what might happen next). For personal change, leaders must measure their behavior and its results. Without solid metrics that specify what should be happening in terms that can be counted and tracked, your aspirations for the organization you wish to lead or the leader you wish to be are just that—aspirations, something that would be nice to have but is not likely to become a reality.

While most leaders would agree that data improves decision making, there are some common mistakes made in using data to drive sustainable improvements, including

- Building scorecards or reports more than predictive analytics
- Using too much or too little data
- Relying on historical data for future trends
- Isolating performance data from rewards
- Collecting data without first specifying decisions that need to be made

For leaders to sustain the right changes, they need to move up an analytics hierarchy from information and reports (What happened?) to analysis and alerts (What actions are needed?) to insights and predictions (What will likely happen next?). To move up this hierarchy, leaders need information about what will happen combined with insight about what could happen. Moving up this decision hierarchy requires metrics that track sustainable change through four principles:

- Move from general objectives to specific measures.
- Measure what's important rather than what's easy to measure.
- Ensure that metrics are transparent and timely.
- Tie metrics to consequences.

General Objectives and Specific Measures

Politicians who get elected tend to make broad promises about sweeping changes they will make if only you vote for them. When they don't deliver on their broad promises, people feel underserved and complain. If they don't deliver at all, they usually get voted out in the next election. Leaders who sustain change ensure execution because they demand that broad and exciting objectives—also known as *visions, missions, values,* and *strategic intents*—translate into specific and measureable actions. At times, leaders proclaim business goals such as doubling in size in the next five years, becoming best in class in customer service, or recognizing people as the most important asset. These general business objectives may be memorable, but until they translate into specific measures, they cannot be turned into reality. Numbers are the language of business, and until leaders learn to put numbers to desired personal or business changes, the promises are likely to stay vague abstractions. Here are some questions that a sustainable leader who wants to double a business can ask to move from general objectives to specific measures:

- Does every part of the organization intend to double in revenue? Or are there some divisions that should grow tenfold or more in the next five years, whereas others might grow more slowly?
- How do we intend to grow? What is the mix of organic growth and mergers or acquisitions?
- What are our assumptions about support organizations? Should we let them double in size to match the doubling in revenue? Or keep them leaner?
- What are the profits-to-growth tradeoffs? Is it growth first and then profit or profit first while growing as fast as possible?
- What leadership and talent developments are required to do this growth sustainably?

If these questions are not answered clearly and with numbers, then the exciting general objective is merely rhetoric. Leaders must translate general objectives into specific measures that will be tracked, or they will hope for change but not lead it.

The same applies to leaders who want to improve their leadership skills. General improvement goals such as listening more, being more strategic, or having more emotional intelligence need to be translated into specific measures. As discussed in Chapter 3, we coach leaders to identify observable behaviors that reflect their improvement goals. These personal behaviors then can be monitored and tracked to help leaders make and recognize progress.

At the end of a performance management discussion, both assessors and assessees need to be very specific about intended improvements. If the assessor leaves the assessee with vague improvement goals, the assessee can never demonstrate progress. If the assessee offers ambiguous self-improvement efforts, they cannot be tracked. The same specificity helps to turn insights from training experiences into actions in daily work.

Measuring What Matters

We live in a world in which data are constantly being gathered about our habits and patterns. Our computers collect "cookies" that report on who we are and what we look at. After staying at a hotel or flying on an airline, we receive online requests for feedback about how we enjoyed our visit. When we use apps on our smart phones, we get requests to provide feedback. It seems that most of the time when we respond to requests for data, nothing really happens other than more placements on junk mail lists for hair-restoring miracles and supplements.

Too often organizations approach data gathering the same way; they collect masses of easily obtainable information and then often ignore it. Think of the impact of employee opinion surveys in most companies. People help to collect, analyze, and report the data, but the only real change is an increase in cynicism about the next survey. Most people know that better information and analytics drive insights that lead to faster and better business decisions. In functions such as finance and supply chain, that's old news. In many organizations today, enormous energy is going into marketing and customer analytics. The challenge is less about accessing data and more about making better decisions. When metrics start by collecting data, they seldom lead to better decision making. When metrics start by being clear about questions they should answer that will enable strategy, the situation is entirely different. Leaders who want to increase productivity, match the right people with the right position, or monitor quality of leadership can use employee survey data to make better decisions.

Too often, however, leaders measure what is easy and not what is right. Right measures align with strategy and turn strategy into concrete, specific indicators that can be tracked. Right measures focus on the future with the information about predicting what will happen and with insights about what works best in a particular setting. Incorrect measures can hurt the business by misdirecting employee attention to focus on the wrong things. Or they can mask real problems as they occur. Leaders who sustain their personal changes have the same obligation to create effective measures that focus attention on what they are trying to accomplish.

Leaders sustain their change when they convert data into meaningful and important measures. The power of predictive analytics that transform data into strategic information is featured in Michael Lewis's best seller, *Moneyball*. Lewis follows the story of Billy Martin, the manager of the low-budget Oakland A's baseball team, whose passion for statistics and numbers helped to contribute to some unlikely results for the team, including a number of victories and records in the early 2000s. The Oakland A's used available player data and converted them into important recruiting information—such as how many times a batter got to first base—while discounting easily obtainable data such as a prospect's size or power, which had much less to say about probable success on the team.

In retail, similar predictive analytics guide customer service. Consider this excerpt from a recent article in the *New York Times* that describes how Andrew Pole, a statistician and marketer at Target, leads a group that converts data into usable marketing information:

> Most shoppers don't buy everything they need at one store. Instead, they buy groceries at the grocery store and toys at the toy store, and they visit Target only when they need certain items they associate with Target—cleaning supplies, say, or new socks or a six-month supply of toilet paper. But Target sells everything from milk to stuffed animals to lawn furniture to electronics, so one of the company's primary goals is convincing customers that the only store they need is Target.
>
> There are, however, some brief periods in a person's life when old routines fall apart and buying habits are suddenly in flux. One of those moments—*the* moment, really—is right around the birth of a child, when parents are exhausted and overwhelmed and their shopping patterns and brand loyalties are up for grabs. But as Target's marketers explained, timing is everything. Because birth records are usually public, the moment a couple have a new baby, they are almost instantaneously barraged with offers and incentives and advertisements from all sorts of companies. Which means that the key is to reach them earlier, before any other retailers know a baby is on the way. Specifically, the marketers said they wanted to send specially designed ads to women in their second trimester, which is when most expectant mothers begin buying all sorts of new things, like prenatal vitamins and maternity clothing. "Can you give us a list?" the marketers asked.

"We knew that if we could identify them in their second trimester, there's a good chance we could capture them for years," Pole told me. "As soon as we get them buying diapers from us, they're going to start buying everything else too. If you're rushing through the store, looking for bottles, and you pass orange juice, you'll grab a carton. Oh, and there's that new DVD I want. Soon, you'll be buying cereal and paper towels from us, and keep coming back."

The desire to collect information on customers is not new for Target or any other large retailer, of course. For decades, Target has collected vast amounts of data on every person who regularly walks into one of its stores. Whenever possible, Target assigns each shopper a unique code—known internally as the Guest ID number—that keeps tabs on everything they buy. "If you use a credit card or a coupon, or fill out a survey, or mail in a refund, or call the customer help line, or open an e-mail we've sent you or visit our Web site, we'll record it and link it to your Guest ID," says Pole. "We want to know everything we can."

Also linked to your Guest ID is demographic information like your age, whether you are married and have kids, which part of town you live in, how long it takes you to drive to the store, your estimated salary, whether you've moved recently, what credit cards you carry in your wallet and what Web sites you visit. Target can buy data about your ethnicity, job history, the magazines you read, if you've ever declared bankruptcy or got divorced, the year you bought (or lost) your house, where you went to college, what kinds of topics you talk about online, whether you prefer certain brands of coffee, paper towels, cereal or applesauce, your political leanings, reading habits, charitable giving and the number of cars you own. (In a statement, Target declined to identify what demographic information it collects or purchases.) All that information is meaningless, however,

without someone to analyze and make sense of it. That's where ...
dozens of other members of Target's Guest Marketing Analytics
department come in.[1]

A week or so after this article appeared in the *New York Times*, *Forbes* ran an article headlined, "How Target Figured Out a Teen Girl Was Pregnant Before Her Father Did."

Take a fictional Target shopper named Jenny Ward, who is 23, lives in Atlanta and in March bought cocoa-butter lotion, a purse large enough to double as a diaper bag, zinc and magnesium supplements and a bright blue rug. There's, say, an 87 percent chance that she's pregnant and that her delivery date is sometime in late August.

An angry man went into a Target outside of Minneapolis, demanding to talk to a manager: "My daughter got this in the mail!" he said. "She's still in high school, and you're sending her coupons for baby clothes and cribs? Are you trying to encourage her to get pregnant?" The manager didn't have any idea what the man was talking about. He looked at the mailer. Sure enough, it was addressed to the man's daughter and contained advertisements for maternity clothing, nursery furniture and pictures of smiling infants. The manager apologized and then called a few days later to apologize again.

On the phone, though, the father was somewhat abashed. "I had a talk with my daughter," he said. "It turns out there's been some activities in my house I haven't been completely aware of. She's due in August. I owe you an apology."[2]

When Arthur Martinez (CEO of Sears) partnered with Tony Rucci, his head of human resources, they worked to correlate employee opinion surveys with customer satisfaction surveys. It turns out that there is a strong correlation between committed Sears employees and committed customers. For every 5 percent increase in employee attitude, there is 1.3 percent increase in customer impression and a 0.5 percent increase in store revenue growth. Conversely, a decrease in employee satisfaction also leads to a decrease in customer delight and store performance. Employee surveys actually could predict customer satisfaction and profitability. Martinez and Rucci found a way to measure something that mattered not only inside the store but also outside with customers.

In each of these cases—Billy Martin at the Oakland A's, Andrew Pole at Target, and Arthur Martinez at Sears—a leader wanted to sustain organization changes through measurements that track not what is easy but what is important. Their focus was on predictive analytics, or finding early indicators that would signal important future changes. For Billy Martin, it was on-base percentage; for Andrew Pole, it was shopping patterns; and for Arthur Martinez, it was employee engagement. Leaders are more able to sustain organization change when they can identify and track early indicators.

For example, at The Home Depot (the world's largest home-improvement retailer), Dennis Donovan launched a human resources (HR) analytics team tasked with supporting the transformation of the business. According to our RBL colleague, Bob Gandossy, who interviewed Donovan, they began their work by collecting employee engagement data and correlating those data with store-level business metrics such as sales per square foot. The team then was able to use those data to test the efficacy of HR program changes such as the skill requirements and recruiting practices at the store level by assessing their impact before modifying and launching these changes more broadly across the organization. This helped to make sure that they were doing the right thing with the broad-based programs, and it also established a clear correlation between key business metrics and the characteristics of incoming employees and the skills of managers.

Another example Bob Gandossy shares is Starbuck's Partner Insights Team, in which a group of Ph.D. and analytics experts was assigned the task of moving beyond backward-looking HR dashboards and scorecards and deriving more predictive analytics related to human capital. Created by Dave Pace, the head of HR at Starbucks, the team focuses on predicting the future when it comes to human capital issues and strategy decisions for the growing Starbucks business. Using sophisticated data mining and modeling techniques, the team is uncovering new opportunities for how Starbucks manages its business and people. According to Pace, the work is building HR's credibility within the organization by focusing on "predictive metrics that have the same impact for HR as financial planning and analysis has to Finance." The team works in tandem with the overall HR operations (called "Partner Resources") to ensure that the workforce of over 100,000 employees is ready and equipped to help the company continue to grow.

In a similar way, personal leadership change is more likely to be sustained when the leader tracks the progress of behavioral change. Leaders wanting to be more customer-centric may track the number of customers they contact in a month, the amount of time they spend with customers, the number of customer complaint cards they review, or the number of customer visits they host at their company. These numbers monitor their behavior so that they can see whether they are making progress. Important measures are lead indicators that show whether desired changes are taking root.

Transparency and Timeliness

Leaders who ensure sustainability make sure that it's clear to their teams what is expected of each player and of the team overall and that all participants know that their performance is tracked and shown in a transparent and timely manner. Without transparent and timely measures, employees don't know where they stand—and they don't know what they are expected to do to improve.

Another personal example: Dave and Norm share season tickets to Utah Jazz basketball games. Dave is an experienced basketball player and fan, whereas Norm is more of a judo/wrestler/hockey type who does not completely understand the game of basketball but loves to go anyway. During a game this season, the conversation turned to metrics. Norm had been focused on the big scoreboard that hangs directly in front and above their seats and reports the overall score, the number of timeouts taken, the number of fouls for each player, and each player's points. Dave pointed him to a smaller scoreboard on a sidewall that he called the "hustle scoreboard." According to Dave, the hustle scoreboard shows which team is trying hardest and is highly correlated with the score. It tracks blocked shots, assists, turnovers, and rebounds. A hustle scoreboard is a lead indicator of what behaviors need to stop, start, or continue to win. A coach who checks the hustle scoreboard immediately knows what the team must do to improve. If the team is not getting its share of blocked shots or is turning over the ball more than the opposition, then it must improve in very specific ways or lose the game. A *lead measure* provides information about what to improve or continue doing.

The big scoreboard is a lag measure. *Lag measures* describe what has already happened—which is also important to know. If your team is behind 11 points in the first half, that is critical information about the past and informs decisions about what must be done next.

Sustainable leaders ensure that their teams have both kinds of scoreboards—one that lets them know what's happened in the past and another that provides lead indicators to tell them where they must improve.

In our experience, most managers are more familiar with lag measures. In many cases, lag measures are the only ones available. The advent of the balanced scorecard broadens measures from financial to other scores, such as employee and customer activity—but it still primarily reports lag indicators such as

- Profit and loss for the quarter
- Employee turnover
- Customer satisfaction
- Project milestones
- Spend-to-budget ratios
- Productivity

So how do you build lead measures, especially when it comes to human behavior? For example, what sorts of lead measures can help to predict increasing empowerment or innovation or any other vague construct?

Two queries often help move the discussion along:

- If we execute this concept successfully, what will we see more of (in terms of behaviors and outcomes for individuals and organizations)?
- If we execute the strategy successfully, what will we see less of (in terms of behaviors and outcomes for individuals and organizations)?

The brainstorming session that results from these queries gives a large list of potential measures, out of which it is possible to define a simple and small set of critical measures. Table 6.1 provides some examples.

Once these behaviors are identified, they can be tracked and monitored. The more-of and less-of exercise also can be applied to personal change. A leader wanting to be more participative may ask peers and subordinates what actions to increase and decrease to demonstrate participation.

Table 6.1 More-of and Less-of Lead Behaviors

	More of	Less of
Empowerment	Members of the team initiate meetings to discuss progress on projects.	Supervisor initiates most meetings.
	Team members give each other constructive feedback when there is a problem or when someone has done a good job.	The boss deals with problems and praise.
	Team members take initiative to deal with a customer complaint and provide a novel solution.	Supervisors handle difficult customer complaints on their own.
Innovation	Many employees propose solutions or improvements to chronic problems about all types of work—administrative, project, processes—and leaders listen and take action on these proposals.	A small number of smart people are the only ones coming up with innovations that leaders listen to.
	Employees make consistent use of our enterprise-wide forum for innovative ideas so that they can go around their boss to get their ideas accepted.	Supervisors determine whether ideas go forward to be implemented, and they quash a lot of good ones.
	Employees engage in experimentation and networking during scheduled free time to come up with innovative ideas and improvements to the work.	Employees work on assigned tasks during work hours.

While coaching, 360-degree feedback, and performance reviews are inherently private or one-on-one meetings between a leader and employee, the outcomes of these conversations can be transparent. In our coaching, we often invite the people we coach to look at the causes and effects of their behaviors. We want them to focus on improving their base behaviors that will have positive consequences. We then encourage them to share publicly with their peers or teams the private commitments they have made.

Tie to Consequences

Consequences are more than a matter of accountability (as discussed in Chapter 4); you can tinker with rewards to ensure sustainable organization and personal change. In reality, if you don't have effective measures, you can't design effective rewards. If you have good measures, good rewards generally will follow. Rewards without measures will only randomly drive sustainability. When strategy translates into measures that then drive rewards, sustainability follows.

Consequences may be broadly defined as negative or positive. Negative consequences imply that missing a standard leads to some form of punishment. Negative consequences generally have a short-term impact, driving behavior because of fear of punishment. When those pressures are removed, the behaviors often return because every unwilling act of obedience was accompanied by thoughts of what would be done if punishment were not imminent. Positive consequences tend to have a longer-term effect on behavior because it's likelier that behavior repeatedly reinforced by desirable results will become a habit.

At a personal level, a friend has a "politician diet" to keep his snacking under control. He selects a politician he does not respect or support. If he fails to lose his target weight in a month, he has to donate $100 to this politician's campaign. He said that he has only missed one month—not only did he feel awful about it, but his donation also showed up on the Internet, and several of his friends teased him about switching political parties.

A teacher can impose negative consequences by docking points from students who are late to class. Students are motivated to get to class on time to avoid the punishment of losing points. Alternatively, the teacher can reinforce arriving at class on time by occasionally opening the session by giving out a few questions that will be on the final exam. Students are motivated to get to class on time in the hope of picking up something that will directly benefit their final grade. They don't just show up on time; they show up without resentment, prepared to listen to the teacher.

At work, negative consequences include taking something away (e.g., salary cuts, dismissal, replacing flexibility with rigid rules) or removing opportunities (e.g., loss of a promotion or job opportunity). Positive consequences vary by individual, providing more of whatever the individual employee wants from the work. People have different needs, and that makes some rewards more valuable than others to any given individual. Some people may be more driven by financial rewards and others by opportunities for impact. These drives may evolve over a career cycle or as a result of other personal factors. Overall, they have a more lasting impact than negative consequences because they focus on the future and what can be, as well as encouraging learning. Leaders are more likely to drive sustainability through positive consequences than negative ones.

Positive consequences can be divided into financial or nonfinancial. Financial incentives can be further divided into cash or benefits, short or long term, base or at-risk pay, and individual or team-based. Nonfinancial rewards generally deal with the work itself or how the work is organized and performed. Financial rewards start with tracking the right measures. The financial rewards need to be tailored to business conditions. For example, if a down business year undercuts an organization's profits, the organization should not give employees money that does not exist. Promising money when it is not available creates discouragement. Rather than focus on nonexistent financial rewards, leaders can productively switch the emphasis to nonfinancial rewards.

Deciding whether to use negative or positive consequences and whether to use financial or nonfinancial rewards depends on the criteria for the rewards. Steve Kerr, a long-time thought leader in the reward domain, has suggested six criteria for effective rewards:

Criterion	Definition (Rewards Are Effective If They . . .)
Availability	Are available throughout the firm.
Eligibility	Are awarded based on clear criteria at each level (hourly, union, executive).
Visibility	Are made known to the recipient and the rest of the organization.
Performance	Vary depending on the performance of the individual or the contingency organization results.
Timeliness	Are allocated close to the time that measurements are made.
Durability	Have sustained impact over time.

Availability implies that the reward supply is large enough to have an impact. When companies have a bonus pool averaging 3 percent of salary it is unlikely that the total available cash will have significant impact on employee behavior. Nonfinancial rewards are more readily available in most cases than financial rewards, which may be constrained by economic conditions.

Eligibility refers to the extent to which groups of employees are included in a reward opportunity. For example, sometimes executives have unique retirement systems not accessed by most employees, who rely on 401(k) or other retirement plans. Nonfinancial eligibility might include such things as attendance at senior leadership meetings. Generally, these meetings are held for the top 1 percent of employees determined by hierarchy. In one firm, we recommended that 20 percent of the slots for this senior management meeting be allocated to employees outside the top 1 percent who displayed high performance in the preceding year.

Visibility implies that the rewards need to be known to both the recipient and the rest of the organization. When rewards are shared only with the recipient, it is only the recipient whose behavior changes, not others'. Public disclosure of salary results creates equity challenges for leaders because those who did not receive the salary increase may feel mistreated, but it also motivates people not receiving rewards to learn what matters most. Again, nonfinancial consequences are often more visible, such as conference attendance, promotions, or assignment to more interesting work.

Performance contingency implies that the reward is connected to meeting standards. No one doubts that financial rewards should be tied to performance; sometimes financial rewards have such a narrow range (e.g., when the company has a salary increase of 3 to 5 percent across the board with a 4 percent average) that they do not reflect the variance in performance. High-performing employees often deliver two to three times the value of lower-performing employees.[3]

Timeliness requires that rewards be distributed close to the time that the performance driving the reward occurs. Annual bonuses require individuals to trust leaders to remember their good performance for the first 10 or 11 months of the year.

Durability refers to the extent to which the reward has impact over time. At times, annual salary increases are seen as an entitlement and are woven into the household budget even before they arrive. Nor can financial rewards be taken back. Nonfinancial rewards, on the other hand, endure because employees have opportunities to change how work is done.

When financial or nonfinancial rewards meet these criteria, change is more likely to occur because it is tracked with consequences. When financial rewards meet the criteria, they drive sustainability. A number of innovations in financial rewards have been adopted that help leaders to meet the recommended criteria:

- *Spot awards.* Leaders in some firms offer on-the-spot bonuses (either cash or stock options or grants) to employees or teams who perform well. These are one-time windfalls for excellent performance.
- *Skill-based pay.* Compensation systems may be based on the extent to which employees master competencies or skills required for their job. These skill-based pay systems are contingent not only on outcomes but also on behaviors.
- *Long-term incentives.* Leaders are finding ways to connect short-term employee behavior with long-term firm interest through stock grants or options or bonuses tied to the preceding two or three years' performance.
- *Pay at risk.* Increasingly, a higher percentage of overall compensation comes from pay at risk instead of base pay. This practice enables leaders to hold constant or offer incremental increases in base pay (which limits the long-term liability of the firm) and offer bonuses, incentives, or other cash gains based on performance.
- *Team rewards.* When the work requires teamwork and measures of teamwork can be crafted, it is useful to allocate financial rewards to the team and not just the individual. Team-based compensation encourages teamwork and collaboration.
- *Customized deals.* Some companies are moving away from traditional "Hay points," where employees receive pay based on know-how,

problem solving, and accountability scores built into their job descriptions, and shifting toward customized employee deals tied to competence and performance. The focus is more on equity (pay for performance) than equality (everyone with a given job description gets paid the same).

- *Benefits.* Employee benefits have financial implications. Leaders are finding new sources of benefits, and they are linking the receipt of these benefits to meeting standards—not just giving them to all employees who meet the eligibility criteria.

As these and other innovations occur, leaders can use financial rewards to ensure sustainability.

Nonfinancial rewards also affect performance. Many of the non-financial rewards show up in the way work is organized. After decades of research,[4] leaders have learned that empowered work has the following features:

- *Autonomy.* Many employees value the right to make their own decisions, to have control over their work environment, and to have a license to act. Autonomy comes from sharing decision making, authority, and responsibility. It may fall to individuals or teams.
- *Feedback.* Many employees like to know how they are doing on the job.
- *Task identity.* Many employees have pride in the work that they perform by identifying with the goals and values of the firm. When these employees have the opportunity to complete an entire task (end-to-end process), they receive value.
- *Task significance.* Many employees want to be involved in work that has an impact on the lives of others.
- *Skill variety.* Many employees want to work on jobs that offer opportunities to learn and deploy new skills and talents. The chance to learn and grow motivates these employees.

Leaders can use an array of nonfinancial rewards as positive and negative consequences for employees who meet or miss standards. Alfie Kohn, who claims that financial rewards don't work, encourages leaders to use choice (i.e., give employees choices about what they do and how to do it), collaboration (i.e., create teams to have a positive social setting), and content (i.e., the five dimensions just listed).[5] Bob Nelson has captured numerous ways to reward employees outside traditional financial incentives in his *1001 Ways* books.[6]

Consequences work. People generally do not act randomly; they act because a positive consequence reinforced the behavior or a negative consequence deterred the behavior. As leaders become clear about strategy and measures, they can creatively craft financial and nonfinancial rewards that change behavior and sustain the resulting patterns.

Conclusion: Leaders as Trackers

At the beginning of this chapter we introduced Abraham, the African tracker. Where we simply saw dirt, he saw unique animal tracks. Abraham did what we elegantly call *predictive analytics* by seeing in the dirt what we did not see.

Leaders also need to be trackers who can see in their data (dirt equivalent) patterns and opportunities. Our tracker would be as lost with leadership data as we were with his dirt mosaic. But leaders who want to sustain change through tracking should move from general to specific objectives; track what is important, not just easy; be transparent and timely; and tie measures to consequences. The test in Exercise 6.1 helps you to see how good you are as a leadership tracker.

Exercise 6.1   Indicators of a Leadership Tracker

Give yourself five points for each item that you mark as something you do consistently.	
1.	I am clear about what results I want to accomplish and what results I want my team to accomplish.
2.	I have created a tracking system that my team is aware of, buys into, and uses to guide behavior, and I use such a system myself.
3.	I translate general objectives into discrete and specific measures for myself and for my team.
4.	I do data mining so that I can turn general data and information into measures that are important.
5.	My scorecards for myself and my team are balanced—it includes financial and softer measures such as employee engagement.
6.	My scorecard includes lag measures of performance—measures that have already happened (profit and loss, employee turnover, customer satisfaction, etc.).
7.	My scorecard includes lead measures of performance—measures that guide my behavior for the future, that is, what people need to do more of and less of to win.
8.	I tie my scorecard and my team's scorecard to consequences that are nonfinancial, such as time off or opportunities to work on other projects, as well as financial.
9.	I prefer to look for quick wins rather than implementing grand plans.
10.	People outside my team perceive us as clear about what success looks like to us and would say that we are continually improving.

If you scored 0–15 points: You are a lost tracker. You don't have a score-card, so any road will take you to where you are going.

If you scored 20–35 points: You are a meandering tracker. You have insight into where you are going, but you are not getting there quickly. There are likely many detours on your journey.

If you scored 40–50 points: You are an expert tracker. You know where you are going and you ensure that you get ongoing feedback to keep you on the path to high performance.

iphone: **RedLaser**
Android: **Barcode Scanner**

Scan this QR code to see how good you are as a leadership tracker.

leadershipsustainability.com/ qr/tracking_assessment

CHAPTER 7

MELIORATION

7

Live as if you were to die tomorrow. Learn as if you were to live forever.

—Gandhi

So far we have described five of seven disciplines that leaders must develop to sustain what they start: They need to find *simplicity* in complexity, ensure sequence and *timing*, demand individual and organization *accountability*, take advantage of internal and external *resources* to support their efforts, and keep *track* to ensure progress in the right direction.

For the sixth discipline we found in our taxonomic research, we have chosen an unfamiliar term with a familiar message. *Melioration* comes from the Latin *melioratus*, meaning "improved" or "strengthened." For leaders to sustain desired changes, they have to *meliorate*, or improve, build on strengths, and learn.

Real-World Melioration

Here are two examples of executives who have found ways to genuinely make things better.

Khalid Al-Kaf, CEO, Mobily

Khalid Al-Kaf is CEO of Mobily, the fastest-growing telecommunications company in the Middle East and North Africa. Mobily launched in Saudi Arabia, a country the size of France, with a license to serve 14 cities in six months. Before the end of that period, the goal had been expanded to 32 cities. Khalid was determined to be lightning fast, and he understood that mistakes could be extremely detrimental. His only competitor was Saudi Telecom, which was firmly entrenched, having begun as a monopoly. Khalid set out to recruit 2,000 staff to ensure high-quality service and to demonstrate a differentiated option to Saudi Telecom.

Two months into the startup (in July 2004), Khalid and his wife traveled from Jeddah to Paris to attend a board meeting. He switched on his mobile phone to make a call from the Jeddah airport and found that he couldn't get service. His wife was still carrying her United Arab Emirates (UAE) phone, which was working. Khalid borrowed it and—after a few calls—discovered that a Mobily cable had been cut and service was down across the entire Kingdom of Saudi Arabia. Khalid's first reaction was anger and a deep concern for the impact this would have on the fledging company. After all, Mobily was his responsibility. As a new operator in Saudi Arabia, he wanted his company's brand image to be boosted—not tarnished by an absence of network service so early in the venture.

Instead of lashing out, Khalid made one phone call to his chief operating officer (COO) and calmly pointed out that they should not panic—the COO simply needed to get a team and fix the problem as quickly as possible. Khalid reminded his COO that if anyone were to be blamed, it would be himself—the CEO. He would not start looking for a scapegoat. The company needed to get service back up for customers; Khalid and his team could troubleshoot why it happened later. In addition, Khalid reminded his COO that they needed to use this as an opportunity to demonstrate to customers that Mobily was different.

By 4 a.m. the crisis was resolved. Mobily workers had been able to connect all the cables, and service was back online. This incident sent a clear message to Khalid's staff and to the board that Khalid was not a blamer; he was willing to take responsibility and believed that the way the company solved problems really mattered.

A few months later, Khalid conducted an after-action review with his top executives. They agreed that this is what they had done and learned during the crisis:

- Rather than make excuses, they faced the problem and sent out a press release explaining that the outage was Mobily's mistake and that the company was going to fix the problem.
- There was some initial debate about the burden of compensating customers for lost service, but the company decided to do it (at a cost of millions of dollars).
- A market survey found that customer perception of quality increased by 35 points from the preceding survey. The highest score was network reliability. This survey was conducted *after* the major outage.
- The impact of the company's approach was to increase trust with customers as a result of its response to fixing the problem. Customers perceived Mobily as transparent, trustworthy, and reliable.
- The company invested in additional infrastructures to undergird reliable service so that the problem would not recur.
- The best result—and one the company could not have bought— was that a few months later, when a competitor had an outage, the press negatively compared the competitor's response to Mobily's standard of service.

This is an exemplary case of melioration. Khalid is responsible and earnest in his desire to learn rather than to blame. He walks into a problem rather than attempting to hide it. He leads a team to take action in a customer-centric way. The result of solving a crisis in this way is better customer relationships and an industry perception that this company is the standard of excellence. This result turned a crisis into an opportunity to differentiate. This is learning and adaptation at its best.

iphone: **RedLaser**
Android: **Barcode Scanner**

Scan this QR code to watch a case study about Mobily, the fastest-growing telecommunications company in the Middle East and North Africa by CEO Khalid Al-Kaf.

leadershipsustainability.com/qr/meliorate

Dave Petersen, CEO, OC Tanner

OC Tanner develops employee recognition and rewards programs that help companies appreciate people who do great work. Its CEO, Dave Petersen, lives in Salt Lake City.

Dave quickly warms to the topic of melioration because he believes that OC Tanner has a long history of successfully applying this concept. OC Tanner's founder, Obert Tanner, had a reputation for visiting the company's manufacturing plants well into his eighties to ask questions about how work was done and to figure out ways to improve productivity. This was 50 years before the concept of continuous improvement.

Most of us remember the anxiety millions of people felt as the calendar turned from 1999 to 2000. This event was pegged "Y2K," and pundits predicted a collapse of computer systems worldwide, asserting that many programs were not prepared for the change in the millennium. Dave recalls how daunting this challenge was for OC Tanner's leaders as they made a "bet the future of the company" investment in their systems.

During this tumultuous period, the company brought in Todd Skinner, a famous "free" mountain climber, to speak to its employees. Free climbers go up mountains without the benefit of ropes and other safety gear. To begin his talk, Todd rappelled off the top of the auditorium and immediately gained everyone's attention. His talk had a huge impact on those in attendance because his approach to mountain climbing was not only an inspiration for tackling tough problems but also an ongoing metaphor for how to live and work.

Todd pushed them to "get on the wall" as the only way to get a difficult situation accomplished. You can't reach the top if you don't start. Sometimes you just have to figure things out as you go. No amount of planning helps more than just going for it and learning firsthand what the real problems are. When you are on the wall, you will find better crevices on the right or left that you can put your hands or feet in that you did not know about before you started. You can expect setbacks, but if you are resilient, you can overcome any challenge.

Ever since this talk, individuals and teams at OC Tanner use the phrase *get on the wall* to figure out tough problems. Dave Petersen feels that this is one of the keys to its success as a company and that few principles have greater impact. As Dave says,

> If we have chronic problems, we get on the wall; if we have competitive challenges or customer challenges, we get on the wall to work them out. This doesn't mean we bypass study or planning, but at some point there is enough defined, and then we have to go for it to get more definition of the challenge. Getting on the wall gives our people the license to try things and sometimes fail but to always get back up and learn from their mistakes. We know this is messy but it works for us.

A few years after Todd came to us, he fell to his death in a climbing accident. As a management team at OC Tanner we talked about his death as a learning experience. We all know there's danger in getting on the wall, but we still have to try, and we have to be safe.

Melioration in the Workplace

Most managers think of themselves as reflective, systematic planners rather than as people who seek constant improvement. In Chapter 3, however, we cited work by Henry Mintzberg, who found that managers continually improvise, adapt, and learn (or meliorate) the non-routine parts of their jobs. The stereotypical image of the rational manager reflects attempts by management writers to systematize managerial work. In fact, the planning that managers do is done implicitly in the context of daily actions. Managers act, respond, decide, and move forward. Managerial rationality is often post hoc, making sense of the work after it has been done.

Others also have explored the idea of managers as improvisers rather than rational planners. Tom Peters called this "ready, fire, aim" and made it the foundation of his 25 years of work on managerial excellence.[1] Kaplan called it "leadership versatility."[2]

These more recent ideas are based on work by Gene Dalton, Lou Barnes, and Abe Zaleznik, who looked at business change, religious conversion, and brainwashing in Chinese thought-reform prisons.[3] They found differences between initiating and sustaining change. To sustain change, people must find ways to make it their own. They must meliorate it in order to truly own it. Ed Schein also reported studies of Chinese thought-reform prisons in which the prisoners were kept under extreme pressure to make a confession of their guilt.[4] But they were not told what the context of their confession should be. Prisoners had to supply the material for the confession themselves. They were only told repeatedly that if they stopped holding back, the pressure would cease. Their task was to produce a confession that would demonstrate to the satisfaction of their captors their complete and unqualified acceptance of the Communist scheme of things. To do this, they had to improvise with material from their own experience. Completely fabricated confessions were usually condemned and rejected. For an acceptable selection and interpretation of this material, prisoners had to look for cues from their interrogators, their fellow prisoners who had successfully confessed, and the controlled mass media. Prisoners had to try repeatedly to demonstrate that they had come to interpret the events in their lives in terms of the constructs of their captors. Having had to use these constructs to analyze their own life experiences, prisoners found the Communist worldview less implausible and foreign. In essence, the Chinese thought-reform prisons forced prisoners to brainwash themselves.

At one level, Chinese thought-reform prisons are a long way from our day-to-day organizational life, and they seem altogether repugnant to consider as a model. At another level, however, the process of figuring out what people want and expect so that we can adapt, fit in, say the right things in the right ways, learn, and get things done reminds us of our first job experiences or our consulting work with new organizations. We have to demonstrate that we understand the organization's context to do our work. The extreme Chinese examples communicate a clear lesson about how to sustain change through a commitment to improve, get better, and learn, or to meliorate.

When we have been asked to describe this process, we use the example of two groups wanting to cross a river. The first group (call them *planners*) doesn't take the first step until it has specified its precise destination on the other bank and has identified each rock group members will step on to reach the destination. The second group (call them *pioneers*) looks across the river to a direction (not destination) and finds the first few rocks its members will step on and get started. The group has a gap between the rocks it sees that its members can step on and the other side, but it moves ahead anyway, confident that it will discover what it needs along the way.

Some architects now build buildings using the pioneer metaphor. Rather than planning everything completely before starting, they often have a general image of the final edifice and then begin the tasks to get there. Like the pioneer crossing a river, these architects have a direction (not destination), and they know the first few steps to get started, confident that they will fill in the gaps.

Leaders who sustain change do the same. They often do not know exactly what the precise end state will be, but once they have enough clarity of direction, they can take the first steps and then meliorate—that is, improve, learn, and get better along the way. In the leadership field, this is often called *learning agility*.[5] Learning agility has been seen as one of the single biggest personal predictors of leadership success. Those with learning agility think quickly, take the initiative, ask questions, make fresh connections, think broadly, and know their personal strengths and weaknesses. Melioration, in our terms, makes these skills an essential part of leadership sustainability because leaders who sustain change are constantly changing the rules of change. They are improving, getting stronger, and learning through four key pioneering principles:

- Experimentation
- Self-reflection
- Improvisation
- Resilience

Experimentation

Most people have routines that they consciously or unconsciously follow. They drive to and from work the same way every day. They eat the same food for breakfast—or they always skip breakfast because they are late. Routines such as this show up in many areas.

For example, there are lots of unwritten rules of conduct about being a good participant in a workshop, conference, and training program. One of them is that people "own" their spot in the room after they have claimed it the first day. Experiment with this conventional wisdom by changing your seat during the day or the next day, and you will likely encounter a hostile glance, an impatient comment, or perhaps even a declaration of territory from the person who sat there first.

Jeff Dyer, Hal Gregerson, and Clayton Christensen argue that there is a difference between discovery and delivery skills among founder CEOs of companies that innovate successfully.[6] Discovery skills allow innovators to come up with new ideas by thinking and acting differently from others. Delivery skills emphasize execution through planning, organizing, implementing, and controlling. Founder CEOs of innovative companies tend to score high in both dimensions, whereas successor CEOs tend to score much higher in delivery skills. So what enables someone to become more innovative and to think and act differently from others? Dyer, Gregerson, and Christensen discovered four individual actions that increase discovery in the innovation process: questioning, observing, networking, and experimenting.

The delivery skills that lead to sustainability have been discussed in other chapters. But even in the discovery process, leaders who experiment encourage sustainability. Experimenting leaders challenge themselves and others to try new and different ways of doing things, to learn from them, and to make them stick. They also run lots of pilot tests with the axioms:

- *Think big.* By thinking big, leaders want to get the largest upside possible. What is the potential of what I want to get done?
- *Test small.* By testing small, leaders run pilots rather than taking big risks. Where can we test this potential with the smallest risk?
- *Fail fast.* By failing fast, leaders learn how the idea, product, or initiative might or might not meet its potential. What are the criteria for success, and how do we encourage success and learn from failure?
- *Learn always.* By constantly staying open to learning, leaders have a mind-set of continuous improvement with both successes and failures. What worked and did not work, and how can we learn from it?

Leaders in a global medical devices company had a major choice about where and how to introduce a new product: Do we start with a big roll-out across Europe and then expand to North America and Asia, or do we start with a small trial in Poland? The decision was made to start in Poland. The intent didn't change. This was still a global roll-out (Think big!), but with a pilot in Poland (Test small!). As expected, the pilot turned up a few glitches, notably how to educate doctors about when to use and when not to use the product (Fail fast!), but adaptations were quickly made so that a successful European regional roll-out could take place within a few months (Learn always!).

We have captured much of what it means to be an experimenter in Table 7.1.[7]

To train yourself to experiment more, try these simple steps: First, read diversely. Carlos Gutierrez, former CEO of Kellogg and U.S. Secretary of Commerce, told us that he read *Rolling Stone* magazine. This is unexpected for a corporate CEO, but not unusual for innovators. Whenever we visit the offices of new executives, it's always interesting to see what they have on their bookshelves. Unfailingly, the most innovative have the most diverse magazines and books lying around.

Table 7.1   Characteristics of Experimenters

Less Likely to Experiment	More Likely to Experiment
Takes the path of least resistance	Likes challenges
Closed, more of an internal processor	Open to ideas of others
General orientation to problems	Specific detailed orientation
Narrow in interests and resources	Many interests and resources
Avoids risks, waits, prefers staying the same, cautious	Accepts personal risks, takes lead in first-time situations, energetic
Closed, low interest in feedback	Asks for feedback, seeks improvement
Focuses on *what* answers and solutions	Focuses on *why* and *how*, seeking new approaches
Planful; follows steps and processes	Resourceful; gets it done somehow
Lives in the present	Comfortable projecting into the future
Doesn't spot underlying patterns	Detects essence
Unable to explain ideas and concepts well	Makes the complex understandable
Prefers a personal solution	Helps others to think through solutions

Second, have broad interests. Dixon Thayer, who we introduced in Chapter 6, has successfully turned around and sold a variety of companies over the last 20 years and is known for his novel approach to making deals work and getting people to work together. Dixon has a lot of unique qualities, but something that stands out to us is his filing system. He has an incredibly diverse set of interests—genealogy, snow skiing, health-care reform, windmills, sailing, junkyards, measurement systems, thoroughbred horses, and many others. In fact, it's hard to find a topic that he can't go to his file system and find something about. He is constantly tweaking, upgrading, and connecting people and things. He is very systemic in his ability to organize himself to try new things—to experiment. His experimenting helps him to see new solutions to old problems and also helps him to learn.

Third, run into and not away from failures. Of the four axioms, "Fail fast" most often stumps leaders. Like people keeping up a money-pit house, leaders persist in investing in projects or products because of their emotional and financial sunk costs. Knowing when to let go of a vision, project, initiative, or personal behavior often requires objective views of subjective investments. Objectivity necessitates honestly examining the initiative and seeing whether it is accomplishing its intent. Having done hundreds of after-action reviews of project failures, we find that most leaders privately admit that they knew months earlier that the project would not succeed as planned, but they were unwilling to admit to failure. We encourage leaders to rejoice in rejection as long as the failure leads to learning that can be adapted in subsequent projects. Shifting from an invest-to-grow to a learn-from-failure mind-set is difficult, but leaders who do so are more likely to sustain changes because they focus on ideas that will work rather than continuing to invest in those that won't. One CEO we worked with would give large bonuses every year to innovators. Half the bonuses went to projects that did not work as intended because he wanted to encourage experimentation, risk-taking, and learning from failure.

The process of experimentation increases sustainability because in trying out new programs, leaders become committed to the concepts behind the program, and when the experiments work or when lessons are learned from failures, people move with dedication to make the program happen.

Self-Reflection

By three methods we may learn wisdom: first, by reflection, which is noblest; second, by imitation, which is easiest; and third, by experience, which is the most bitter.

—*Confucius*

During stressful times, one of the most effective ways to relax and learn is to engage in self-reflection. During one particularly stressful time not too long ago, Norm's wife Tricia was sitting at a doctor's office contemplating her situation and what could be done about it. Over several minutes, the contemplation turned to the outside window of the doctor's office, where a medium-sized black spider was climbing slowly up the white-painted wall of the building. The self-reflection slowly turned to an "Aha" moment as the spider became a metaphor for just putting one leg in front of the other to keep momentum going. *I am the spider. Don't give up. Just keep climbing.* This seemed to be an answer from heaven. Keep moving. Don't give up. Be the spider.

From out of nowhere, a praying mantis appeared, grabbed the stunned spider, and disappeared with the spider in its grasping claws. Self-reflection turned to anger. *The mantis just killed my spider. How unfair.* The spider was an inspiration. So, if the message was to be the spider and the mantis just ate the spider, what is the lesson now that life is an existential journey toward certain death and destruction? This further self-reflection turned to laughing out loud. The "Aha" moment shifted to not plodding forward but to enjoying the moment. There are things we can't control in life. While the spider was plodding up the wall, the mantis was looking for lunch. In addition, our black spider was not too smart walking up a white wall. Both lessons of plodding forward and enjoying the moment were equally valid— but for now the important one was to simply enjoy the moment.

At one level this story is funny because the spider was killed right after it became the metaphor for constancy and refusal to give up in pursuit of change—only to be subject to the greatest change of all. At another level, neither of these insights would have occurred had Tricia not taken the time to self-reflect. No matter what happens, self-reflection leads to some kind of useful learning.

At his trial for heresy, Socrates said, "The unexamined life is not worth living." He was on trial for encouraging his students to challenge the accepted beliefs of his time and think for themselves. The sentence was death, but Socrates had the option of suggesting an alternative punishment. He could have chosen life in prison or exile and likely would have avoided death. But Socrates believed that these alternatives would rob him of the only thing that made life useful— examining the world around him and discussing how to make the world a better place. Without his "examined life," there was no point in living. So he suggested that Athens reward him for his service to society. With his response, the city leaders had no alternative and were forced to vote for a punishment of death.

Luckily, leaders today are allowed and encouraged to examine their professional and personal lives through self-reflection. Psychologists, drawing on Buddhist traditions, call this *mindfulness*— where people work to become acutely aware of the realities around them. Often the hard part of self-reflection is to find the time to build it into a life filled with activities and ruled by crowded to-do lists. However, without self-reflection, life may be shallow and hollow; with it, life becomes an opportunity to meliorate and get things done.

Self-reflection helps individuals to sustain change because it replaces avoidance with reality. Psychologists have done more than 6,000 studies that show confronting negative self-images and then replacing them with positive ones leads to effective behavioral change.[8] Table 7.2 sets out some specific ways that leaders can reflect that help them sustain the changes they intend to make.

Table 7.2 *Positive and Negative Self-Reflection Thoughts and Actions*

Positive Self-Reflection (Reality-Based)	Negative Self-Reflection (Self-Deceived)
What could I have done to frame this so that we could make a decision?	The rest of the team never makes decisions in these meetings.
I wonder what I did that caused her to say that.	I can't believe that she said that to me; I wasn't the one responsible for the loss of that customer.
What information can I give them to help them understand the situation?	They don't know what they are talking about.
Could I have been more specific in my communication?	He always gets lost in the details.
How can I connect with people who disagree with me?	I am not talking to him about it;... he is always on the wrong side of the issue.
What is really going on with him? What does he really mean?	He always says one thing but means another.
What can I do to help her get this done?	If she doesn't deliver, this won't get done.

Leaders who practice self-reflection constantly observe themselves and want to improve how they come across. They ask themselves some of the following questions to help them see how they are doing:

- What insights have I gained about myself from what just took place (in that meeting, conversation, presentation)?
- Could I have misinterpreted some insights about myself? Do I need to test my insights?
- Have I discovered a specific attitude or behavior problem that leads me to be less effective than I want to be?
- When I try something new and succeed, why has my new approach been more effective than my traditional one?
- Am I consistently able to apply what I've learned when similar situations occur?

Through self-reflection, leaders can become aware of themselves and how they come across to others.

One of the ways a leader can build the discipline of self-reflection is to write. Writing forces us to articulate and go public with what we think. The writing may include a daily journal to capture day-to-day insights, a white paper to take a position on a topic, a blog post about what's important to you, or a letter (or e-mail) to a friend. The important thing is to write. Best-selling author Julia Cameron encourages "morning pages" every day as a quick way to clear your mind of isolated and random thoughts.[9] She claims that this enables creativity and the ability to focus and get things done. Writing solidifies learning by requiring clarity about what we believe and by forcing us to take a scripted position on an issue. Sustainable leadership increases through writing. Some writing tips:

- Find a place that is comfortable to write, and build a discipline to write there at the same time every day. If you are writing to self-reflect, it's helpful to avoid distractions such as loud music or a TV show in the background. We prefer to write in our home offices but have disciplined ourselves to write during long airplane rides.

- Start asking yourself questions that you want to have answered. Before we wrote this section on self-reflection, we went through a preparation process. We talked to others about their stories of self-reflection. We did "fingertip research," using a search engine to discover what others have written about it. We asked ourselves and each other why we agree or disagree with the experience of others. We formed a hypothesis about self-reflection and what is most meaningful to share.
- Push yourself to be honest with yourself. Do I really believe what I am saying, or am I saying this because it's what others have said? When we get excited about an idea, it's because we find a different way to look at an idea that has impact. There is a gut feeling that there is truth in what we are saying, and we are open to being wrong until we test it. Self-reflection writing is true to who you are.
- Draft and edit, and then keep editing. The hardest part of writing is the effort to put something into words for the first time. After that, you are refining the idea. The refinement leads to examples and better ways of saying it. But if you don't write it the first time, the self-insight doesn't come.
- Take sustainable action. Johann von Goethe said, "Never by reflection, but only by doing is self-knowledge possible to one." This seems to contradict our initial point about self-reflection, but it does not. The purpose of any reflection is to improve the ability to do something. Sustainable leaders use self-reflection not only to relax and gain insight but also to frame actions that work.

Self-reflection allows leaders to meliorate. This process also enables them to sustain change because they possess a mind-set of constant learning.

Improvisation

In earlier work we have used the metaphors of a jazz ensemble and a symphony orchestra to describe the difference between improvising and detailed planning.[10] A jazz group plays from a lead sheet, whereas a symphony plays from a score. The orchestra score is a very detailed plan about what the composer intended the music to sound like when it is played. The members of the orchestra must follow the conductor's lead to implement this plan to perfection, bringing each instrument into play at the proper moment and with the proper notes. The lead sheet is much less detailed. Basically, it lays out the melody of the music—we are playing "Turkey in the Straw" or "Happy Birthday." The intent of the jazz group is to improvise complex sounds from the simple lead sheet rather than contribute to a predetermined intent. So the orchestra starts out with a complex design and asks people to follow directions. The jazz group starts simple and becomes more complex as members improvise to wow the audience.

Philosophically, the orchestra score intends to eliminate mistakes by clarifying which instrument is to be played at which precise time and by whom. Jazz improvisation doesn't regard variations in such matters as mistakes because whatever happens is part of the learning experience. The players in the jazz group try to "get into a groove" by playing music that the audience likes. Musicians take turns improvising around the intent of the music and know that they are successful when it sounds good and they get an enthusiastic response from the audience. The audience at an orchestral concert is supposed to be quiet, and both small mistakes and exquisite execution are obvious to an experienced listener. Someone who makes a vocal response to either while the music is playing will be asked to leave. Table 7.3 compares the effectiveness criteria of an orchestra with those of a jazz ensemble.

Leaders who improvise and follow the jazz metaphor are more likely to sustain their leadership changes because change is

Table 7.3 *Effectiveness Criteria for Orchestra and Jazz Ensemble*

	Orchestra	Jazz Ensemble
Strategy	Complex score: Follow directions. • Detailed and intricate • Composer writes • Conductor interprets	Simple lead sheet: Improvise from central idea. • Simple • Low detail • Bottom up
Structure	Functional: Wind instruments together in one section, percussionists in another, and so on.	Cross-functional: Musicians gather in a loose group, regardless of instrument.
Leadership	Conductor, top down	Shared
Customers	Audience is quiet and listens with a critical ear.	Audience gives real-time feedback so that group can respond.

inherent in what they do. The orchestra score and the lead sheet represent the strategy or goals of the team. The audience represents customers. Leaders with an orchestra mentality tend to engage in more formal, planned actions, whereas those with a jazz mentality proceed on more of an ad hoc basis. Some of the differences in the kinds of actions they take are set out in Table 7.4.

In the orchestra, the conductor is the leader, and in the jazz group, the leadership tends to be shared. The jazz group often features a leader who has superior skills. However, even a famous jazz musician such as Wynton Marsalis still jams with his group in a way that features all of them. Although years of management theory would indicate that the conductor of the orchestra is the ideal leader, we'd argue that a leader who wants to sustain change also should consider the value of being a good jazz leader. The good jazz leader or the jazzy

Table 7.4 *Orchestra versus Jazz Ensemble Management Actions*

Orchestra-Style Management Actions	Jazz Ensemble–Style Management Actions
Classroom	Mentoring
Virtual classroom	Job shadowing
E-learning	Simulations
Knowledge management	Communities of practice
Document approvals	Social networks
Learning portals	Forums and bulletin boards
Job aids	Wikis
Creating baseline knowledge	Blogs
Dealing with compliance and risk	Instant messaging
Improving organization efficiency with standard tools and approaches	Modeling desired attributes
Aligning learning with strategic goals	Providing real-world experience
Capturing and disseminating institutional knowledge	Practicing in a safe environment
Efficiently addressing common knowledge gaps	Collaborating to create solutions to complex problems
Minimizing time requirements through efficiency analyses	Creating flexible and innovative options

business leader ensures that everyone knows the intent of the strategy. There is an understanding that things will change over time in ways that no one can plan. The jazzy leader encourages others to improvise when conditions change—basically to come up with unplanned actions to deal with these changes. Improvisation increases the ability of the leader to keep things simple while allowing for complex actions to deal with changing circumstances.

Improvisation is not the right solution in every circumstance. For example, you don't want your heart surgeon to start improvising when preparing for surgery. On the other hand, you do want your heart surgeon to be able to improvise if something goes wrong during the operation.

Improvising leaders also tend to do better with customers. Orchestra leaders tend to follow the rules and keep inside the boundaries of what has been set out for them. When a problem arises, orchestra leaders restate the rules. Unfortunately for such leaders, customers want to receive a product or service in a manner that optimizes their experience with it and tend not to care about its producer's rules. Improvising by listening to the customers' needs and translating that information into actions that matter to customers is a key sustainability skill.

Last year, Norm's daughter Ashley got married with much help from Norm's wife, Tricia. One evening, Tricia and Ashley spent hours choosing shoes for the bride and her six bridesmaids on the Zappos website. Their plan was to order many combinations of shoes, have them sent to their house, where the bridal party could try them on, and then send back the shoes not chosen. Unfortunately, when they were finally satisfied, they pushed the online order button and nothing happened except that their hard work disappeared from the screen into the twilight zone. Ashley wept. Tricia ranted.

Luckily, they had kept paper notes and called Zappos to shout at someone—and the someone they reached was an improvising Zappos customer service rep. In her most disgusted voice, Tricia described the problem, including the plan to order several combinations of shoes that would be returned. The Zappos rep did not hesitate. He declared, "I'm so sorry this has happened. What an awful problem to have when you are so excited about your wedding. Of course, we understand that you would try on the shoes and send them back. How else could you figure out the ones you like! We are going to make you a VIP member today. As a VIP member, you get overnight shipping free of charge and your returns are free."

Still Ashley and Tricia were suspicious. It couldn't be this easy. The next day a box arrived in the late morning with a large vase and an amazing bouquet of flowers. The note read: "Congratulations to the Mother of the Bride and Welcome as our newest VIP member." By midafternoon, the shoes arrived. By late afternoon, the customer service rep called to see if everything had arrived. By early evening, Tricia and Ashley were writing online testimonials about Zappos. Not a bad outcome for Zappos from an incident that started with a faulty online order button.

Improvising leaders get sustained results. Tricia and Ashley will buy more of whatever Zappos sells.

iphone: **RedLaser**
Android: **Barcode Scanner**

Scan this QR code to see Tricia Smallwood tell about her experience with Zappos.

leadershipsustainability.com/qr/zappos

Resilience

We often do an exercise about personal leader brand where we ask people to pick three words or phrases that describe them. To keep it interesting, we often ask people to do this exercise for another participant they know well. The words Norm uses for Dave are

- Learning … commitment to inquiry and new ideas
- Ideas with impact
- Autonomy

The words Dave uses for Norm are

- Resilience
- Entrepreneurial
- Application of ideas with impact

Norm finds it flattering to be considered resilient until he begins to reflect about it. Resilient people fail more than others. They are resilient because they try things, fail, and then are able to deal with the failure. On even deeper reflection, resilience puts Norm in some great company. In 1979, Godfrey Hounsfield (the Nobel Prize winner for medicine) was asked the secret of his success. His reply: "I grind up more pig brains." In effect, Hounsfield is saying that he is more resilient—willing to try more things that turn out not to work. His payoff for his resilience was the Nobel Prize for a breakthrough in radiology imaging.

Hounsfield's first experimental system used gamma rays from the radioactive element Americium to scan bottles or Perspex jars filled with water and pieces of metal and plastic and was "very much improvised," as he recalled in his Nobel lecture. A lathe bed provided the means for moving and rotating the gamma-ray source, and sensitive detectors were placed on either side of the bottles or jars. The scanning process took nine days and created 28,000 measurements, which took a high-speed computer two and a half hours to calculate and process. The images the computer created, though, were good enough to convince both Emergency Management Institute EMI and the Department of Health to invest £6,000 each in the acquisition of an x-ray tube and a generator, which would reduce scanning time to nine hours. Hounsfield traveled across London by underground bringing bullock and pig brains fresh from the abattoir to his laboratory, and he produced the first pictures in which white and gray matter could be clearly differentiated.[11]

Resilient people get sustainable results because they are willing to carry brains across London on the underground. Resilient people keep trying until they succeed. That is sustainability.

Another story of resilience captured a global audience. Thirty-three miners were trapped in a mine in Chile. These miners communicated with their families through small tunnels that rescuers drilled into the mine where they were trapped.

Prior to the tunnel drilling, the miners had been underground for 17 days, living off limited reserves in one of the mine's emergency shelters. The nine-inch tunnels were barely big enough to pass messages, food, water, and basic supplies through.

The rescue mission to free the men from the mine took 69 days; during that time, they lived without light or sanitation. It's hard to imagine the hardship the miners and their families experienced. However, during their final rescue, their only disagreements were about who should come up last. A community of resilience had developed during the hardship that led to genuine acts of selflessness. This group of miners kept trying, even though the odds were against them, and the result was a successful rescue. In this case, the resilience of the rescue workers also must be noted.

Most of us aren't going to win the Nobel Prize in medicine or be faced with living for months 700 meters underground trapped in a mine. But we all face setbacks during the course of our lives. It's these small setbacks that accumulate and turn resilience into despair and finally giving up.

Leaders who sustain change through resilience recognize that change is not a linear process from point A to point B. As in crossing an uncharted river, resilience requires taking risks and experimenting, reflecting on what does and does not work, improvising, and ultimately being resilient enough to continue. This cyclic process of sustained change means that each iteration improves on the preceding one—that the learning, or melioration, becomes a discovery process that cannot readily be put into a spreadsheet. The 33 men, trapped for 17 days before they had contact with the outside world, had to exhibit enormous resilience. In French, the word for resilience is *rebounder*, or "to bounce back." Resilient leaders bounce back when things go wrong rather than becoming discouraged and giving up.

The ability of leaders to bounce back and sustain changes they desire comes from personal, social, and organizational resilience. At a personal level, resilient leaders have a positive outlook on life and see what is right, not what is wrong. Like Godfrey Hounsfield, they persist because they believe in their cause. They have humor and the ability to laugh at themselves, as well as the humility to accept counsel from others. They fortify their attitude and draw on what works in their life rather than what doesn't. They build on what is good and right, not on what is wrong and unjust. They are able to put things into perspective and keep at it. At a social level, resilience increases when leaders expand their friendship circles by intentionally meeting and working with new people. Instead of isolating themselves, they work to connect with others from whom they can learn and grow. At an organization level, resilient leaders meliorate by facing problems early (Fail fast!) and by doing regular and rigorous after-action reviews to learn about what did and what did not work. They encourage discussion of the things that might be most difficult to discuss, tend to be transparent and open with information and decisions, and offer others opportunities to learn and grow.

A senior leader we admire once said that he often made the 55/45 decisions, that is, decisions with a 55 percent clarity of what needed to be done and a 45 percent lack of clarity. He said that someone else who reported to him should make the 90/10 or 80/20 decisions. We think that leaders who want to have an impact should focus on difficult and demanding decisions. But in the process, these leaders often make wrong decisions. As this leader told us, "If the decision is too obvious, I should not make it. I make the decisions where the answer is not obvious, and unfortunately, I am sometimes wrong." Resilience means that the leader meliorates or constantly works to learn and improve.

Conclusion: Leaders as Pioneers

Effective leaders are pioneers who seek a direction not destination and move forward with values to reach the direction. Like jazz improvisers who make beautiful music, leadership pioneers start with a simple idea and experiment with it to make it work. In Roman mythology, Sisyphus was punished by being required to roll a boulder up a hill, only to have it roll down again. His endless and unavailing trial was to labor without making progress. Had he known the discipline of melioration, he might have experimented more, been more self-reflective about what was and was not working, improvised ways to find alternative solutions, and been resilient enough to keep trying. Some leaders have enormous mountains to mount, be they customer expectations, employee commitment, financial results, or personal change. If these leaders can act like pioneers who improve, get stronger each iteration, and continually learn, they meliorate. By so doing, they sustain their desired changes in themselves and their organizations.

CHAPTER 8

EMOTION

8

"All the knowledge I possess everyone else can acquire, but my heart is all my own."

—Johann Wolfgang von Goethe

We all have emotional experiences that linger in our memories. We have deep memories of the birth—or death—of a child, of our graduation day, and of working hard to achieve a sought-after reward and gaining or failing to gain it. Positive or negative, such emotional experiences stay with us for the rest of our lives. In the United States, people remember details about where they were when they heard that President John F. Kennedy had been shot (Dave was in class in grade school, it was a sunny day, and the adults all around him were in tears) or when Neil Armstrong walked on the moon (Norm was on a camping vacation with his family in Aiken, South Carolina, it was a humid night in July, and everyone was watching Walter Cronkite on TV, mesmerized). These memories, and similar ones in other countries (July 22 in Norway, 9-11 for much of the world), are deeply etched into both subconscious and conscious thought because they are imbued with emotion.

Real-World Emotion as a Driving Force

Many people are leery of emotion and inclined to act as though life would be better if only they and those around them could act with perfect rationality. But perfect rationality is rarely the ideal response—at every level, it generally turns out that people make better decisions and pursue them with more vigor when their emotions are engaged. Here are two leaders in two very different walks of life who find that emotion makes them stronger and more effective.

Bill Ford, Chairman, Ford Motor Company

In the late 1990s, Bill Ford was a relatively new chairman of the board for Ford Motor Company. The son of William Clay Ford (brother of Henry Ford II and grandson of Henry Ford I), he was in his early forties with enormous responsibilities. Bill Ford was a board member when multiple change initiatives within Ford were on the table, including allocation of resources, focus on expanding Ford's involvement in the automotive value chain (which many believed took attention away from the core business), controversial management appointments, and new ways of evaluating performance, that many employees viewed as destroying the historic Ford culture. With no indications otherwise, and with a Ford at the top, employees believed that the family must support the changes. The company historically had been a place for lifelong careers over generations of employees, but many were openly questioning the wisdom of such a choice.

On a morning in February 1999, the unthinkable happened. A cloud of smoke appeared in the sky over the Rouge Complex, at that time still one of the largest vertically integrated manufacturing sites in the world. Explosions had rocked the Rouge Power Plant, a facility operated by Ford employees within the Rouge Complex to produce power for many of the site's operations. Word quickly reached leaders in Ford's World Headquarters building, including the chairman,

Bill Ford. The smoke could be seen from his office, and he feared the worst. So his immediate reaction was to go to the Rouge to do something to help. His lieutenants advised against going, citing personal danger and unwanted media exposure. He would hear none of it and made the short drive from Ford World Headquarters to the Rouge.

What Bill found was every bit as serious as he had feared. Damage to the power plant was extensive; people were being carried out of the building on stretchers and assisted by uninjured employees and firefighters. The cause of the explosions and the extent of the destruction were not fully known at that time, so tensions were high about the dangers of further problems. The media was reporting the incident as breaking news—disaster at the Rouge. But Bill did not shy away from the media. He didn't go to a controlled meeting space to be interviewed, choosing instead to stay with his people. When the media approached him for comment, he didn't give a public relations message. He spoke from the heart about this tragedy, about the hardworking people of Ford being hurt, and about getting them help, and he called it "the worst day of my life." His comments were honest and emotional.

The news media covered the event for days. The video clip of Bill Ford's comments was used extensively. What viewers saw was a man who represented one of the wealthiest families and one of the best-known companies in the world. They saw him distressed like a father who was mourning a family loss, who was a real person, who cared deeply about his employees. Viewers saw the real man during a time of extreme distress—through his emotional reaction to an event. This was someone you could trust. This was a leader you wanted in your world.

In a few minutes, therefore, the persona of Bill Ford changed. He became the father figure of the broader "Ford family." He stayed personally involved in finding causes of the accident, he partnered with the United Auto Workers (UAW) and Ford manufacturing leaders to put a new emphasis on safety in all company facilities, and he listened to people about the impact of changes that ran counter to the emotional ties that employees had to Ford. During this process, from the accident and media coverage to policy changes, Bill built credibility with his leadership team, with employees, and with union leaders—particularly those in the UAW. The company was in a downward spiral for many other reasons at that time. Bill took over the CEO role personally, replacing Jac Nasser. Over the next few years, Bill rebuilt a leadership team that halted the downward spiral and laid the foundation for recovery.

Buzz Nielsen, Chief of Police, West Valley City, Utah

West Valley City has the second-largest police department in Utah. Its chief, Buzz Nielsen, is a graduate of the FBI Academy's executive program and a former vice president of the Utah Chiefs of Police Association. He has been with the department since 1980, working in a variety of roles, including narcotics, homicide, and hostage negotiation, before taking over.

Police work can grind people down and lead them to detach themselves from emotional life. It hurts to care when you're dealing constantly with people in pain (or with people who put other people in pain), especially when limited tax dollars restrict your salary and other resources. But Nielsen cares. His decades of experience have not eroded his personal values or his willingness to connect with individuals on an emotional level, and he sets a standard that his whole department picks up.

Police forces tend to become communities in themselves, and Nielsen blends work and outside time with his people, doing everything from playing golf to helping remodel their houses, to build strong positive emotional ties among them. His contribution as chief is crucial—he looks for ways to build a culture that is focused on the individuals in West Valley City rather than on the internal workings of the police department. He reminds his officers that the work they do really makes a difference to the lives of those they serve and that they need to find ways to connect to citizens as individuals and neighbors.

He encourages them to listen, and he listens himself when people reach out to him directly—even though that's not part of his usual job. When someone called him in frustration, saying that her neighbors, the school authorities, and the local policemen all agreed that she was looking at something suspicious, but there was nothing to do but wait and see, he agreed that perhaps there ought to be more. The problem, she said, was the house next door, where a constant stream of teenagers arrived at all hours and stayed only a few minutes before they left—unlikely social visitors for a thirtyish couple with three little kids. It looked like drug sales to her, and no one was suggesting a reasonable alternate explanation.

Of course, when people complain that they believe a neighbor is committing a crime, the police can't just barge in—they have to have a concrete reason to check things out. But Nielsen felt that he couldn't just sit back and wait either. He told his officers to find opportunities to show themselves—to take lunch breaks or write up reports while parked in front of the alleged drug dealer's house, for example. The road is public property, and the officers did not accuse anyone of anything; they just sat there working. But the ploy had less impact than expected, at least on the house's clientele. Teenagers continued to come to the house, though the officers were interested and entertained to hear the home owner screaming at them to go away—couldn't they see the police car parked in front of the house?

Based on this, Nielsen stationed an unmarked car near the closest stop sign, less than a block from the house. The officers watched people leaving the targeted house, waiting for someone to speed or roll through the intersection without coming to a full stop. On the second day, they pulled a young man over for a "California stop" (where the car does not stop completely) and asked some pointed questions. The offender seemed disoriented and appeared to be chemically impaired, so they searched his car—finding several bags of methamphetamines, which he confessed he had just purchased at the house the officers were watching.

That afternoon, a SWAT team broke down the door of the house and discovered a meth lab in the small and unventilated basement. The children were taken to waiting social services professionals, and the parents were arrested and taken to jail.

When the story broke, the original caller phoned Nielsen again and repeated over and over how much she appreciated the dedication of her city police and their willingness to listen to her concerns rather than ignore her. Nielsen shared the praise with his people, and her response added to the high of the successful raid to reinforce the West Valley City department's sense of mission.

And it's a tough mission they have, combining serious crime fighting with caring and going the extra mile to build connections with the community. The members of the department share an organizational purpose that is more than just doing their job—they are helping others make a difference within their community, and that makes a huge difference to them, too.

iphone: **RedLaser**
Android: **Barcode Scanner**

Scan this QR code to watch a case study of Buzz Nielsen, the Chief of Police in West Valley City, Utah.

leadershipsustainability.com/qr/emotion

Powering Growth with Emotion

Emotions may be about mood, temperament, personality, disposition, or motivation. They energize, focus, and magnify behavior. Emotions have a neurologic base that can be found in the limbic system of the mammalian brain. Scholars in psychology, sociology, and economics have tied emotions to cognition (how we think and process data), social setting (how we work with others), and decision making (how we take risks and make choices).[1] *Emotional intelligence* is when we are self-aware of our emotions and how they affect others. *Emotional well-being* is when we know how to shape our circumstances to enhance our emotional energy.

Leaders who want to sustain behavioral change are more likely to succeed when the desired behavior is aligned with their emotions. It is estimated that as much as 80 percent of decisions are made by emotion, yet when they hope to improve their decisions, leaders tend to focus more on knowledge than on feelings.[2] When coaching, training, performance management, or 360-degree sessions include emotions, not just facts, leaders personalize and claim the changes they intend.

We have identified six principles of emotion, each of which leads to a personal question leaders can answer to increase their emotional commitment to sustain personal change:

- *Have clear reasons.* Why do I want to lead?
- *Identify energy enhancers.* What gives me emotional energy and well-being?
- *Connect change with personal values.* How do the leadership changes I want to make tie to what I believe?
- *Connect change with organizational purpose.* How do I tie my leadership changes to what we need to accomplish?
- *Recognize my impact.* How do my leadership changes affect others?
- *Celebrate success.* How do we communicate and celebrate our accomplishments?

When leaders recognize and balance emotional energy with rational information and facts, they are more able to sustain changes in themselves and others.

Have Clear Reasons

Ask yourself, Why do I want to lead? One leader we coached was being vilified in the media. His company had missed earnings projections for multiple quarters, product innovation was lagging, and he was struggling to change his company's culture. Yet he was enormously dedicated and worked hard to turn his company around and transform it. He told us that after one particularly grueling day, his wife greeted him on coming home, almost with hopeful glee, by asking, "Have you been fired yet?" Her good humor implied that if he was fired, she would be a steadying force in his life and, in fact, the emotional burden on him might be lifted. He was not fired, chose not to quit, and eventually did help to transform the company into a new generation of success.

Every leader has to ask, "Am I willing to pay the price of leadership?" We have talked to leader after leader who has paid the price in its many forms:

- *Visibility and loss of privacy.* As leaders move up their organizations, both their public and private actions become more visible. One leader said that he wanted simply to put on his grubby clothes and wander the streets of his city, but he knew that he had an obligation to his company, and his dingy dress would soon show up in derogatory light in a YouTube video.
- *Unfair and extreme criticism.* Leaders have to make difficult decisions, some of which inevitably harm others. As leaders move up the organizations, their decisions become more and not less controversial. In Chapter 7 we noted that leaders have to make the 55/45 decisions (the hard choices) and delegate the 80/20 (the easy ones) to others. Sometimes employees and others criticize hard choices without fully appreciating their context. And, by making the 55/45 decisions, leaders will inevitably make wrong choices. Their ability to face and learn from these choices evokes a personal price.
- *Misunderstanding intentions.* As leaders become more successful and visible, their intentions are more likely to be misunderstood. In particular, since salaries are public and leaders have higher disparity gaps between their income and average income, employees may attribute self-interest and greed to leaders when it is not intended.

- *Isolation and loneliness.* A leader who was popular among her peers was delighted with her promotion. Before long, however, she realized that because of her new role, she had to readjust her relationships with her former peers. While they continued to respect and admire her, she ended up being less of a friend and more of a boss. Leadership is often a lonely job because even those who want to be friends may be seen as seeking favors more than offering personal support.
- *Sense of responsibility and ownership for decisions.* In a party game, one of our friends was asked, "Name your ideal job." When she said that she wanted to be a tollbooth operator, we cringed, thinking of the tedious aspects of that job. Then she explained, "I see all of you bringing your work home with you. Your 8- or 10-hour workday is really 18 to 20 hours because you even wake up worrying about the things you have to do. As a tollbooth operator, I could leave my work at work and be peaceful at home." Leadership requires intensity and personal sacrifice.

The price of leadership needs to be counterbalanced with the benefits and opportunities of leadership:

- *Ability to make a difference on topics and with people you care about.* Asked why he had worked so hard in his job, one leader spoke of the people he worked with. He felt that he could create something that would bless the lives of former, current, and future employees and their families.
- *Ability to shape an agenda.* Leaders find passion in the ability to build something unique and creative. This exists at the top of a company, where a leader has the chance to form and grow an organization, but it also occurs for the leader of a marketing group who targets a new market segment, a technology leader who implements an innovative technology system, or a finance leader who takes pride in managing the capital structure of the company. Leaders set rather than react to or implement an agenda.

- *Ability to grow something that endures.* One of the ultimate tests of leadership is what happens after the leader departs. Good leaders leave something behind. Leaders can often take pride in having established something that endures beyond their tenure.
- *Ability to gain a sense of self-worth.* A leader we coached found a sense of emotional well-being and pride in being an officer of the company. Her role at work gave her a sense of position and status in her community and became a part of her identity.
- *Ability to influence others.* Some leaders appreciate and are driven by power, or the ability to influence others, not necessarily to control them. Leaders appreciate their positive impact on the people they lead.

Personalizing and weighing these costs and opportunities becomes less factual and more emotional. Leaders have to have an emotional (and often irrational) sense of their identity as leaders for them to sustain their energy and enthusiasm. Simply stated, when the costs of leadership exceed the benefits, leaders will not sustain their passion.

In addition, not everyone can or should be a formal leader. In many people's minds and in many companies' career planning, individuals succeed when they move up the leadership hierarchy, gaining increasing accountability and responsibility for managing others and shaping the direction of their organization. In our work, we advocate a two-pronged approach to personal and professional careers (Figure 8.1). Individuals can make a choice about going through a progression of managerial moves (left side of the Y above "Master" in Figure 8.1), or they can choose to remain dedicated to gaining technical mastery and influence (right side of the Y in Figure 8.1). Not all individuals have the skills or inclination to be traditional leaders; many are more comfortable mastering their technical skills and influencing through deep knowledge insights.

Figure 8.1   The RBL career development model.

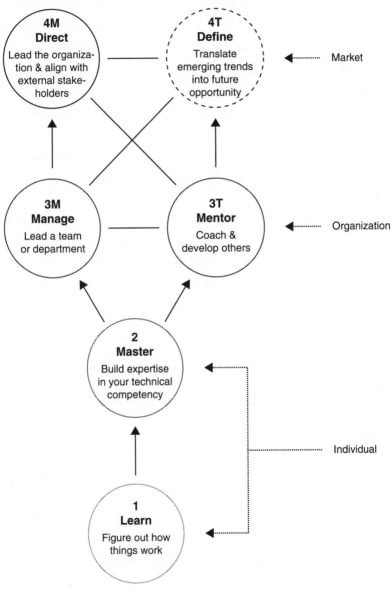

In one case, a technically gifted leader had become CEO of his company to a great extent because of his technical prowess. As CEO, though, he continually tinkered with (his view) and intruded on (his employees' view) the technical work of the company. His deep dives into technical areas distracted him from his proper work of shaping the business and contributed to a learned helplessness among his employees. When he recognized that his true passion and skills were in the technical areas, he resigned as CEO and reassigned himself as a senior technical expert (top right in Figure 8.1). He was not able to sustain his desired leadership changes because they were not right for him to sustain.

Candor about the personal price of leadership and about matching personal interests with the right career track help to sustain leadership behavior. A meaningful coaching or performance improvement question is, "Why do you want to improve as a leader?" The answer to this question should be more emotional than intellectual.

Identify Energy Enhancers

Ask yourself, "What gives me emotional energy and well-being?" Think about the last time you woke up early in the morning excited about work. Something was going to happen that captured your subconscious and helped you to prepare for the day. That something might be a presentation, meeting, project, client visit, or some other activity that emotionally engaged you. In such cases, work generates more sustained energy than all the vitamins, power drinks, and pill supplements that promise to boost vitality.

When people find meaning, passion, or well-being in their work setting, they are more than engaged—they have a sense of contribution. In the marketing field, Philip Kotler talks about the evolution from a focus on product (work to sell product and gain market share) to customer (work to identify and connect with the customer to gain customer share) to values (work to make the world a better place and gain emotional share). Likewise, in the field of positive psychology, Martin Seligman and his adherents have recognized that real happiness has evolved from pleasure (sensual enjoyment) to engagement (being lost in the flow of an activity) to meaning (connecting the activity to deeper values).

This sense of a connecting work activity to deeper values has been studied as well-being, abundance, positive organization, meaning, flourish, and emotional energy. Collectively, these studies explain why people work and how their work creates personal meaning for them. Table 8.1 lists some of these drivers of meaning. When leaders find meaning in the new behaviors they adopt, the behaviors are more likely to endure.

The key factor lists in Table 8.1 may vary somewhat from one another, but they capture the essence of what gives leaders (and others) a sense of meaning at work. When leaders connect the behaviors they want to change with the factors that most create meaning for them, those behaviors become imbued with emotion and are more likely to endure. Such leaders have more sustainable emotional energy at work because they realize that their work connects with their sense of purpose.

A leader we coached wanted to improve his strategic thinking skills, so we worked with him to find ways to assess the external world in which he operated, to make conscious choices about how to allocate resources to align with external opportunities, and to craft strategies and plans to mobilize his organization. Intellectually, he was prepared to be a better strategist. When we talked to him about what gave him meaning at work, however, he talked about his desire to have an identity as someone who was respected for his insights and prescience. We quickly linked his ability to do strategic thinking with his desired identity, helping him see that as he shaped strategy, he

Table 8.1 *Drivers of Meaning at Work*

	Daniel Pink	Tom Rath (Gallup)	Martin Seligman	Marshall Goldsmith	Dave and Wendy Ulrich
Core book	*Drive*	*Well-Being*	*Flourish*	*Mojo*	*Why of Work*
Core premise or question	What motivates people?	What would your best possible future look like?	How do people find happiness in their lives?	How do you find a balanced life and career?	How do people find abundance in their professional and personal lives?
Key factors	Autonomy Mastery Purpose	Career Social Financial Physical Community	Positive emotion Engagement Relationships Meaning Accomplishment	Identity Achievement Reputation Acceptance	Identity Purpose Relationships Work environment Work challenge Learning Delight

also would form and reinforce his personal identity. His passion for strategy went from his head to his heart, and he was able to sustain his commitment more effectively because it became part of what gave him personal meaning at work.

The leaders who find well-being and meaning from work are the ones who sustain their desired changes. It is not that their work gets any easier; in fact, it is often harder, but the personal meaning helps to sustain the changes.

Connect Change with Personal Values

Ask yourself, How do the leadership changes I want to make tie to what I believe? One of the most difficult talks Dave has ever presented was to a worldwide leadership meeting of a large company. More than 500 leaders were assembled to review the business trends, strategy, and organization requirements for success. Dave had about 30 minutes to review ways to turn strategy into action. He did not know much about the speaker before him, except that he had retired recently. When this executive stood to speak, a hush fell. It turned out that this executive had been with the company more than 35 years and was known and beloved by everyone in the room. About a year before, he was diagnosed with a difficult cancer that ravaged his body and caused him to retire. He was near death but miraculously recovered. He shared his personal affection for those in the audience and his enormous gratitude for their faith and prayers on his behalf and for their unending support. He talked about leadership being less about setting strategies and meeting goals and more about nurturing and caring for those in need of care, like himself. He acknowledged these leaders and urged them to take personal pride in their company because they appreciated people as much as profits. He spoke from the heart and connected with their hearts. He roused the emotions of the audience and left them standing for many minutes as they paid tribute to his leadership, courage, and personal connection.

Dave then walked to the podium and said, "Who wants to talk about strategy?" The contrast between an intellectual message of the x steps from strategy to results and the emotional appeal of the preceding speaker were striking. Dave's ideas were organized and logical; the retired executive's message was meaningful and powerful. Emotion and relationship provide a far stronger connection with an audience than expertise for most listeners. Dave did not get a standing ovation.

For leadership change to be sustained, it needs to touch the heart as well as the head. This means that the desired changes should be connected with personal values. Leaders who make change from the heart bring a passion and energy that is beyond a scorecard to a personal cause.

The work of connecting behavior change with values begins with clarifying values. Leaders can discern and detect their values through a number of exercises. They can select values from various lists.[3] They can ask themselves questions about their values and go through reflection exercises such as these:

Diagnostic Questions

- What would I want someone to say about me when I am not in the room?
- What excites and energizes me at work?
- Who am I when I am at my best?
- What are the top three things I want to be known for by those who know me best?
- If I saw a blog about me as a leader, what would I hope it would say?
- What do I hope is said about me at my retirement or funeral?

Reflection Exercises

- Name a time when you felt personally fulfilled because you had done something well. What had you done? What values did you reflect by this activity?
- Write a story about your leadership style that might appear in a business periodical. What values are embedded in the story?

All these clarification questions and exercises help leaders to articulate what they truly value. Leaders who can identify, prioritize, and articulate their most salient values are more likely to be grounded in what matters most to them. But until these values show up in action, they are not real. Connecting actions with values may come from the question, How will my desired behavior change reinforce and support my deepest values?

When behavior and values are in conflict, behavior often wins because it is short term, visible, and current. If behavior trumps values, however, then over time the values become less grounded, less real, and more likely to dissipate and shift. Leaders who connect their behaviors with their values can do so with the *so that* question. In Figure 8.2, list three or four behaviors that you hope to implement and three or four key values that you have. Using the *so that* question in the middle, connect the behaviors with the values. Is this line connecting behaviors with values solid (i.e., clear and unequivocal) or dotted (i.e., ambiguous and sporadic)? The more clear you make this line, the more likely the behaviors are to endure. For example:

- I value *integrity* so that when I tell people what I want, they will know that I am sincere.
- I value *honesty* so that I tell the truth even when it's difficult to say and for the other person to hear it.
- I value *courage* so that I make difficult decisions even when it may be easier to take another path.

Figure 8.2   *Connecting behaviors and values.*

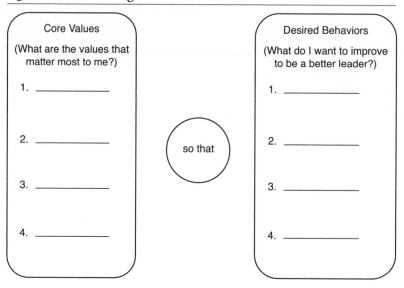

By connecting personal changes with personal values, a leader makes the change more emotional and personal. Richard North, CEO of IHG (an international hotel chain), faced takeover from a corporate raider who began to buy IHG stock in an effort to take over the company and make radical changes. North knew that he wanted to fight the takeover attempt to protect the company and to better serve employees and customers today and shareholders in the future. But when he got underneath his motives for being too aggressive against the takeover, he realized that he was passionate about one of his real values of autonomy and controlling his own (and the company's own) destiny. Remaining independent was not only an intellectual challenge, but it also became an emotional cause for North and his management team. This emotion helped him to share his passion for independence with employees and investors who felt his underlying fervor to fight the takeover challenge. His emotional charge helped to communicate and secure their sustained independence.

The leader who spoke about winning his fight with cancer and Richard North both personalized their intentions by linking them with their personal values.

Connect Change with Organizational Purpose

Ask yourself, How do I tie my leadership changes to what we need to accomplish as an organization? Tying actions to personal values helps to make them sustainable, but actions also can be tied to higher organization purposes. In mission-driven organizations, leaders find it exciting to use the shared mission to encourage and sustain leadership change. Matt Holland, the university president introduced in Chapter 4, wanted his administrators and faculty to be more dedicated to the needs of students. He asked current staff to publicly share stories about faculty who had influenced them to go into the teaching profession, as well as stories of student progress through the university, and to personally mentor a student who welcomed the arrangement and keep students at the center of their teaching and service work. A hospital administrator offered a similar challenge with the mantra of patient care by constantly reminding staff of their noble purpose in healing and saving lives. A CEO of a defense contractor reminded employees of their organization's central role in the security of their nation.

In each of these cases, leaders used the natural higher purpose of their organizations to drive and sustain leadership change. When leaders and employees have a line of sight between their personal values and the organization's purpose, they are more likely to sustain their commitment. The opposite is also true. When personal values come in conflict with the organization's purpose, leaders or employees will not sustain their passion for work. And some companies really need employees to agree with or at least accept the company's purpose in order to sustain their commitment. A tobacco or spirits company, a fast-food company, a defense contractor, or a drug company doing embryo research needs to make sure that leaders who work at the company are at least comfortable with the organizational purpose. If not, these leaders will not sustain their enthusiasm for their jobs, nor the behavior changes they need to make to improve.

Linking personal passion and organization purpose need not occur only in mission-driven organizations. Creative leaders create rallying purposes that capture the emotions of their employees and of themselves. Here are some effective mission or vision statements:

Avon: To be the company that best understands and satisfies the product, service, and self-fulfillment needs of women—globally.

DuPont: The vision of DuPont is to be the world's most dynamic science company, creating sustainable solutions essential to a better, safer, and healthier life for people everywhere.

Heinz: Our *vision*, quite simply, is to be *"the world's premier food company, offering nutritious, superior tasting foods to people everywhere."* Being the premier food company does not mean being the biggest, but it does mean being the best in terms of consumer value, customer service, employee talent, and consistent and predictable growth. We are well on our way to realizing this Vision, but there is more we must do to fully achieve it.

Pfizer: We will become the world's most valued company to patients, customers, colleagues, investors, business partners, and the communities where we work and live.

Qualcomm: To deliver the world's most innovative wireless solutions.

Volkswagen: Our strategy pursues a clear objective: By 2018, the Volkswagen Group is to be the world's most successful and fascinating automobile manufacturer—and the leading light when it comes to sustainability.[4]

For non-mission-driven companies, the vision can still be articulated in such a way as to capture the hearts and minds of leaders and employees. Employees who have a sense of personal pride in the vision of their organization will be more likely to work hard to make that vision a personal reality. We believe that a compelling purpose increases productivity 5 to 10 percent because people have an emotional commitment to their work. These "firms of endearment" create a share of heart that helps deliver emotional and social value and that helps leaders sustain the changes they desire.

Recognize My Impact

Ask yourself, How do my leadership changes affect others? Leadership never occurs in isolation. Leading when you're all alone is like clapping with one hand. Leadership has to occur through connecting with others. Leadership is a team sport, as we pointed out in Chapter 5. Likewise, emotions are not generally created or displayed in isolation, but with and through others. Frustration, anger, discouragement, optimism, joy, and enthusiasm generally occur when interacting with someone else.

Today's leadership vernacular emphasizes "building on your strengths." The logic behind this comes from outstanding work by Martin Seligman, who with his colleagues defined and shaped the field of positive psychology. Instead of focusing on what is wrong with individuals, they emphasize what is right. Instead of overcoming depression, they offer clients ways to find authentic happiness. Instead of diagnosing pathologies and overcoming them, they want to identify strengths and build on them. In *Character Strengths and Virtues: A Handbook and Classification*, a book written with Christopher Peterson, Seligman and his colleagues have identified 24 generic strengths that individuals might possess in six domains[5]:

- *Wisdom and knowledge.* The ability to acquire and use information about the world (creativity, curiosity, love of learning)
- *Courage.* The ability to accomplish goals in the face of opposition (persistence, vitality, integrity, bravery)
- *Humanity.* The ability to tend and befriend others (kindness, social intelligence)
- *Justice.* The ability to experience a healthy community life (fairness, teamwork, social responsibility)
- *Temperance.* The ability to protect against excess (forgiveness, humility, self-control)
- *Transcendence.* The ability to connect to a larger universe and provide meaning (gratitude, hope, playfulness)

A strength is simply something that we find easy, energizing, and enjoyable. Seligman's premise is that when you do well in what you identify as a strength and capitalize on it—rather than trying to shore up your weaknesses—you will have more success and more positive experiences. You'll find happiness. (You can take some of his strengths tests online at www.authentichappiness.sas.upenn.edu.)

It is very hard to disagree with this logic. Marcus Buckingham and others have argued that discovering what we do well is a first step to lasting success. Leaders whose strengths are around creativity will be more successful in innovative organizations and work environments, for example.

But building only on your strengths is not enough if those strengths do not create value for those you lead. In college, Dave majored in English and developed a knack for reading novels. He could read two or three novels a week and found this easy, energizing, and enjoyable. But what he has since found is that few people care about his novel-reading strength. What they really care about is his ability to analyze a situation in ways that help them to reach their goals. Reading and interpreting good writing are sustainable strengths when they inform his ability to diagnose and help others to work through their problems.

According to a recent movie, *The Bucket List*, the Egyptians believed that the gatekeepers of heaven ask new arrivals two questions about their lives on earth: Did you find joy? Did you bring joy to others? The first question is about building on your strengths. It is necessary but not sufficient. It is about the self, not others. The second question shifts the focus of joy to helping others find it. Put in terms of the current discussion, this means that we should build on those of our strengths that strengthen others.

Leaders can strive to develop strengths of authenticity, judgment, emotional intelligence, credibility, and other noble attributes, but unless and until they apply these strengths in ways that create value for others, they have not used the strengths to drive emotional connection. When personal strengths are used to strengthen others, the strengths and actions are much more sustainable. Some in the strengths movement have missed the conclusion Seligman reached in his 2003 book, *Authentic Happiness:* "The meaningful life: using your signature strengths and virtues *in the service of something much larger than you are.*"[6]

For leaders, this means that it is not enough to do our work well. We also must use our strengths to deliver value to others. When we do so, the emotional content of our actions becomes much higher, and these actions likely will endure. In practice, this often means that leaders share emotions with those they lead, that they speak from the heart as well as the head, and that they help others to find emotional energy from the leaders' actions. In coaching, 360-degree reviews, or performance improvement discussions, it is not enough to help the leader improve personal behavior; it is necessary to help the leader recognize how the improved behavior will benefit others.

Emotional bonding with others also helps leaders to sustain change because such bonds support leaders when things go wrong. During times of stress, emotional connections mean more than transactional connections. For example, one leader we coached found that his deep emotional bonding with his team helped him to face some difficult challenges. His people sent him private messages of encouragement—and they also took out an ad in the local newspaper that expressed support for him. The emotional bonds helped the leader to remain constant in his desired change efforts.

Doris Goodwin Kearns studied the unique leadership style of the renowned American president Abraham Lincoln. He had a knack for gaining emotional support not only from his allies but also from his enemies. She identified eight emotional strengths he possessed:

- *Empathy.* He was able to put himself in the place of others so that he could appreciate their point of view.
- *Humor.* He told great stories to illustrate his beliefs, and he often used self-deprecating humor to connect with others.
- *Magnanimity.* He forgave others and was not likely to hold grudges.
- *Generosity of spirit.* He was willing to publicly take the blame when things went wrong, and he admitted mistakes openly and honestly.
- *Perspective.* He put events and activities into context rather than being overwhelmed by an individual event.
- *Self-control.* When frustrated, he would write letters to himself and then tear them up. He thought and reflected before he acted.
- *Sense of balance.* He was able to take time to relax, entertain friends, and let go of the stresses of his office.
- *Social conscience.* He frequently looked for opportunities to serve and work for others.

Leaders who not only recognize their personal emotions but also use their emotions to connect with others are more likely to sustain their desired changes.

Celebrate Success

Ask yourself, How do we communicate and celebrate our accomplishments? When we visit organizations, we become cultural anthropologists whose aim is to discover how employees actually work, interact, and live. We look at multiple signals of an organization's underlying values, including the physical arrangements of office space, the places where employees hang out, and how employees celebrate success. Sometimes offices and celebrations are sterile, with little personalization or revelry. At other times offices and celebrations communicate a sense of emotional connection between employees and the organization.

Leaders who want to sustain personal change in themselves and others can do so more effectively through public celebrations. These celebrations acknowledge and reinforce progress and signal what matters most. These celebrations have emotional appeal. Most of us would not want to drive a pink Cadillac, but for a Mary Kay Cosmetics consultant, the pink Cadillac symbolizes and celebrates success. Those who earn the right to use a pink Cadillac generally don't lose it because the public reinforcement helps to sustain the success that earned the car.[7] southwest Airlines has a similar legacy of celebrating success that started with the legendary antics of its founder, Herb Kelleher, and continues to the current day, with its second round of reality TV highlighting employees who dealt with demanding passengers and its commercials celebrating baggage handlers. Leaders who publicly celebrate their changes are more likely to sustain them because of public pressure.

Will Bowen, author of *Complaint Free World* (Amazon.com, 2007), wanted to help people complain less and be more positive. His celebration exercise is to wear a band on one wrist for 21 days as a reminder not to complain. If you complain about something, the wristband goes on the other wrist. The wristband is a daily reminder of a commitment to change. It is a visible celebration of having succeeded or failed. A company we worked with adapted this approach and asked employees to leave their wristbands on their left wrist each day they went without complaining or being negative about the company but to shift the wristbands to the right wrist if they complained or were negative. The company found a remarkable shift to more positive conversations as people clung to their ability to celebrate success.

Successful celebrations are more likely to sustain change when they are public, immediate, and meaningful. These celebrations may be around an event such as a birthday or holiday or around delivering a business result (e.g., a customer sale, commercialization of a product, or meeting a social responsibility goal). A celebration builds emotional commitment and helps to sustain a desired change.

Leaders who appropriately share their emotions build stronger relationships with their employees. Some leaders work to hide their feelings and avoid becoming too personal with others. These leaders end up distancing and isolating themselves. Leaders who are emotionally vulnerable and transparent will be more likely to sustain change.

A leader we coached was working to be less demanding and more engaging with his employees. As he began his change, he met with employees and shared not only what he was working on but why. He became quite personal as he apologized for his controlling behavior, publically recognizing that it had not been appropriate, and asked for his team's help in alerting him when he fell back into old patterns. This more personal and emotional appeal was counter to this leader's style, but his employees began to trust it because he encouraged feedback on how well he was accomplishing his more engaging leadership behavior. An employee told us that when the leader publicly apologized, something shifted in her relationship and personal commitment to her boss. She felt that if he could be vulnerable and open, she would work to help him reach and sustain his goals. After about 90 days of successfully demonstrating the new behavior, his team surprised him with a cake to celebrate his efforts. This rather minor celebration reinforced that they appreciated the progress he was making. They reciprocated his emotional appeal with their emotional celebration, and it was not surprising that he continued to make progress.

Emotional connection also comes when leaders share credit for success and take blame for failure. One of the signals we look for in leaders who build emotional support is how they talk about their success: Do they say "I" or "we." We listen to leaders' feelings about their accomplishments and remind them that as they share credit for business results, they will reinforce and build success. We have encouraged leaders to share credit for success by writing thank-you notes to an employee's spouse, parent, children, or partner. This sharing credit helps leaders to feel an emotional bond with their team and sustains the success.

Conclusion: Leaders as Meaning Makers

When change shifts from the head to the heart, it is more likely to be sustained because people genuinely care about it. Leaders who want to make personal behavior changes are more likely to do so when those changes draw on emotions by building on meaning and values. Leaders also are more able to drive sustained change when they allow their emotions to become part of their communication and celebration efforts.

CHAPTER 9

CONCLUSION

9

"There is no real ending. It's just the place where you stop the story."

—*Frank Herbert*

Leadership sustainability has become the responsibility of all leaders: leaders charged with building other leaders, human resources (HR) professionals who create the infrastructure of leadership development, and external coaches and advisors who inform the leadership process.

We strongly, yet cautiously, believe that good leaders can become better when they consciously sustain the changes they know they need to make. Most of us learn to parent by copying how our parents parented us. Many leaders lead by mimicking how their mentors and prior leaders led them. Sometimes, these multi-generational leadership efforts work well. At other times, today's leaders need to lead for current, not past realities. Each generation parents better when they consciously improve on the previous generation. Likewise, each generation of leaders also can improve on the past by adapting the 7 disciplines and 31 principles synthesized in this book.

This chapter is designed to help you diagnose your personal leadership sustainability and find ways to improve it—something even the most effective leader can always do. You can use the nine-step "Leadership Sustainability Application Tool" that forms the bulk of this chapter (and is found online at www.leadershipsustainability. com) to help you make sure that your desired changes last. Leadership sustainability occurs when leaders accept *why* they need to improve, recognize *what* they need to improve, and figure out *how* to make the improvements stick. Organizations can enhance leadership sustainability by practices designed to build the next generation of leaders into people who will consistently and completely deliver against strategic goals.

Diagnosing Your Leadership Sustainability

Leadership sustainability is not just a personal trait that makes some leaders inherently better than others. It is a set of disciplines that leaders can consciously master to help them do what they know they should. For each of the seven disciplines that constitute leadership sustainability, we have identified a metaphor that captures what effective leaders do to sustain their desired change:

- *Taxonomist.* Sustainable leaders create simple taxonomies by focusing on the critical items that have the largest impacts.
- *Time logger.* Sustainable leaders manage time as their most critical resource, using their calendar to make sure that they really devote their attention to the things that matter to them.
- *Responsible adult.* Sustainable leaders take personal and public responsibility for their actions and are accountable for the results they get.

- *Teammate.* Sustainable leaders work together to combine unique resources into collective results through coaching and systems.
- *Tracker.* Sustainable leaders track their progress to know how they are doing and to see how today's actions will predict tomorrow's outcomes.
- *Pioneer.* Sustainable leaders constantly learn and grow, being resilient in the face of failure and humble in the face of success.
- *Meaning maker.* Sustainable leaders recognize the value and power of their own emotions and build emotion and meaning in others.

Leaders who make improvements that become part of their normal behavior accept all these roles and apply the principles for each of the seven disciplines. To see how well you practice the 31 principles of leadership sustainability now, complete Exercise 9.1—being as detached and impartial as you can (or have someone who knows you fill it out about you).

iphone: **RedLaser**
Android: **Barcode Scanner**

Scan this QR code to see how well you practice the principles of leadership sustainability now.

leadershipsustainability.com/qr/ postassessment

You can plot your discipline scores on Figure 9.1 to determine your profile of strengths and weaknesses as a sustainable leader. If you score low (below 5) in any of the seven areas, the principles and practices for that discipline may be the ones that would do most to help you improve.

Exercise 9.1   Assessment of Principles and Actions for Leadership Sustainability

Leadership Sustainability Discipline (Metaphor)	Principle and Practice (To What Extent Am I Able To…)	Rating: Low Medium High. 0 1 2 3 4 5 6 7 8 9 10	Average Rating for Discipline
Taxonomist (simplicity)	Focus on what matters most.		
	Tell stories with impact.		
	Avoid concept clutter.		
		Total: _/3 =	
Time logger (time)	Take a regular calendar test.		
	See myself as others see me.		
	Recognize routines.		
	See triggers of lead indicators.		
	Start small.		
	Manage signals and symbols.		
	Be consistent.		
		Total: _/7 =	
Responsible adult (accountability)	Take personal responsibility.		
	Go public.		
	Be consistent with personal values and brand.		
	Hold others accountable.		
		Total: _/4 =	

Teammate (resources)	Use a coach.	
	Build the HR infrastructure.	
		Total:_/2 =
Tracker (tracking)	Move from general to specific measures.	
	Measure what's important and not what's easy.	
	Be transparent and timely.	
	Tie to consequences.	
		Total:_/4 =
Pioneer (melioration)	Experiment.	
	Self-reflect.	
	Improvise.	
	Be resilient.	
		Total:_/4 =
Meaning maker (emotion)	Have reasons to lead.	
	Identify energy enhancers.	
	Connect change with personal values.	
	Connect change with organization purpose.	
	Recognize my impact on others.	
	Celebrate success.	
		Total:_/6 =

Figure 9.1 *Profile of your leadership sustainability strengths and weaknesses.*

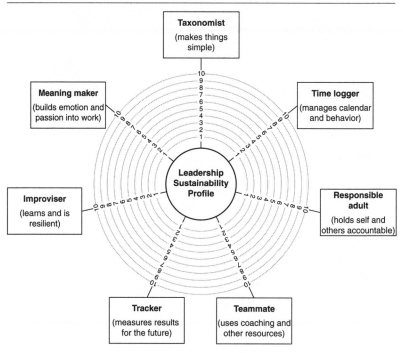

This exercise and profile diagram also can be applied to your work unit or organization. Often organizational intentions (e.g., strategies, goals, priorities, or objectives) are more rhetoric than resolve, more intention than commitment, and more aspiration than action. While this book focuses on personal leadership sustainability, the same 7 disciplines and 31 principles apply to leading organizations. We have seen many companies do a better job at planning than performing, proclaim great aspirations that don't turn into actions, and propose more change than they manage to sustain. The logic we have used in this book can easily be adapted to an organization setting to help sustain desired organization capabilities.

Leadership Sustainability Application Tool (for electronic version see www.leadershipsustainability.com)

To create leadership sustainability, we propose a comprehensive application tool.[1] At the end of most personal leadership improvement efforts, participants recognize why they need to improve and what they need to improve, but even with the best of intentions, they fail to make it happen. Like children who become better parents by changing their parenting narrative, leaders who consciously recognize their leadership strengths and weaknesses can also improve.

Nonetheless, we have worked with thousands of leaders who have accomplished the changes they intended because they successfully adopted the process described here. Our Leadership Sustainability Application Tool takes leaders through nine steps that supplement formal and informal settings where plans for leadership improvement are conceived. In coaching sessions, for example, after the coach diagnoses areas for improvement and articulates personal improvement goals, taking 15 to 30 minutes to review the tool's steps helps to turn coaching insights into active commitments.

Likewise in performance reviews, most discussions of feedback focus on how people can behave differently to reach their potential. Once such behaviors are identified, it is useful to shift the conversation and spend 15 to 30 minutes on the nine steps so that the performance plans are implemented successfully.

In leadership training events, aspiring leaders learn what they can do to be more effective. Most of these changes revolve around specific behaviors that participants should implement on their job. When these learned behaviors pass through the nine steps of the Leadership Sustainability Application Tool, they become vows that are likely to endure over time. This application exercise may take from 30 to 90 minutes with a group, but it is time well spent.

In informal settings, when leaders observe others' behavior they hope to imitate or make personal resolutions to upgrade their behavior, they can use this application tool to ensure that these desires come to fruition.

The application tool asks leaders to answer self-reflection questions for each of the nine steps in Figure 9.2. Some tips for responding to these questions follow the figure. Note that steps 3 through 9 all bear on figuring out how to accomplish the adjustments identified in the process of determining why and what to improve. The leadership sustainability profile in Figure 9.1 provides some useful insights for the process. That is, you should build on your strengths as shown there but not depend on them. To successfully sustain desired improvements, you also need to attend to your weakest areas and pay attention to the related steps. Our recommendations for principles and practices to improve that role may prove especially valuable.

Step 1: Why

Key question: Why is this the right time for me to improve my personal leadership effectiveness?

In all insights and models of personal, institutional, or societal change, the desire for change has to exceed the resistance or barriers to change. Recognizing why change should occur is an inherently personal choice. Most of us have had well-meaning friends or family members recommend that we change when we were not emotionally or mentally ready to make that change. Spending less, taking more time with family, listening to understand, eating less, exercising more, driving more safely, and other changes that others want from us will not happen until we personally feel that it is time to change.

Figure 9.2   Flow of the Leadership Sustainability Application Tool.

Step 1: Why	Step 2: What	How
Why is this the right time to improve my personal leadership effectiveness?	What should I do to improve my personal leadership effectiveness?	How do I rate on each of the seven disciplines of sustainability?

Step 3: Simplicity

Focus on the critical priorities that will make me a better leader.

Step 4: Time

Manage my calendar to reflect my priorities to improve.

Step 5: Accountability

Make sure that I am personally and publicly accountable for making my improvements last.

Step 6: Resources

Get the coaching and institutional support I need to be a better leader.

Step 7: Tracking

Monitor my progress now and in the future.

Step 8: Melioration

Constantly improve by learning, being resilient, and growing.

Step 9: Emotion

Find personal passion and meaning in my improvement efforts.

Leaders may go through formal efforts to help them change, but until they personally recognize that they are prepared and ready to change, it isn't likely to happen. Coaches, assessors, and leaders themselves need to ask themselves the following questions to assess their readiness for sustained leadership change:

- Have I received some specific feedback that I should improve?
  - 360-degree results
  - Performance review

- Coaching
- Experience that did not work
- Training program
- Is there a career opportunity that asks more of me?
  - New position or role
  - New job assignment
  - New task
- Is there a business imperative that demands more of me?
  - New strategy
  - New customer requirements
  - New financial requirements
- Tradeoffs: Am I ready to undergo the emotional demands of change?
  - Why is this a good time for me to become a better leader?
  - Why is this not a good time?
  - What will I have to give up to make these new behaviors work?
  - Am I willing to let go of some things in order to learn new things?
  - Am I emotionally ready to focus on implementing these new behaviors?

Out of these questions, leaders who think about change can discover their sincere readiness for making change happen. Their readiness will help them to answer the question, How committed am I to becoming a better leader? Without an emotionally and intellectually affirmative answer to this question, it is not worth proceeding. In Chapter 2 we discussed the brilliant speech by Dr. Martin Luther King and highlighted the "I have a dream" mantra that defined his speech. But before repeating "I have a dream" so often, he said "now is the time" five times. The "now is the time" mantra embodies a sincere and real commitment to improvement.

Step 2: What

Key question: What should I do to improve my personal leadership effectiveness?

As discussed in Chapter 1, to be effective as a leader, you need to pay attention to both the *leadership code,* or basics of leadership (i.e., strategy, execution, talent management, human capital development, and personal proficiency), and the *leadership brand,* or how to behave to be consistent with your organization's stakeholder expectations. But a human being has only so much attention to pay—it's like time: You can't do everything, and you can't consider everything that might be considered either. The first step toward winnowing the flood of possibilities and identifying what will make the most difference is to monitor the implications of your own choices. When you observe patterns of your behavior and the consequence of those patterns, you can begin to see what you should change. To take a personal example, Dave has observed that in his workshops, participants sometimes have a hard time following the logic and flow of his materials. To minimize that confusion, which was interfering with the effectiveness of his teaching, he now explicitly outlines the workshop and reminds participants where he is in the outline.

You also need to attend to data beyond your own observations. Self-reflection needs to be supplemented with data about how others interpret your behavior. We encourage leaders to use frequent data-collection tools, which might include a formal 360 (or 720) degree process or an informal online comment sheet. We also encourage leaders to pay attention to patterns rather than attempting to analyze outliers in the data. Patterns may be common messages from different people or common messages over time. From these data, you should be able to see what you can do to be more effective.

Relationships also can offer personal feedback to help you know how you are doing. Collegial feedback is one of the best gifts anyone can offer a friend, so encourage it—and offer it, setting an example from which you can benefit. When feedback is delivered with a desire to help, when it is concrete and specific, and when it is focused on the future, it helps leaders to know how they can improve. It's not necessarily comfortable to learn of dysfunctional leadership behavior, any more than to learn that you have mustard on your chin or an unzipped zipper, but it's far better to know than to proceed in ignorance. Sustainable leaders appreciate those who offer advice on how to improve.

In determining what to do to improve, consider the following questions:

- What do I want to be known for as a leader?
- What do I think I need to become to be a more effective leader?
- What are the impacts of these improvements on the various settings where I work, play, and live?
- What will be the outcomes if I make these changes? What will be the consequences if I don't make them?
- What leadership behaviors come naturally to me (my leadership strengths)?
- What do I need to do that is outside my comfort zone to be a more effective leader?

These questions will point you toward the behaviors you need to master to become a better leader.

Step 3: How—Simplicity

Key question: How do I focus on the critical priorities that will make me a better leader?

Sometimes the list of things leaders should do to improve is too long, unfocused, or generic to be helpful. No one can improve all things at once. For example, Norm—a golfer with natural athletic ability—has never had formal golf lessons. When he first met his golf coach, the coach noticed a long list of bad habits. But rather than overwhelm and discourage Norm with all the things he could do to improve his swing, the coach focused on a few priorities at a time—and it's starting to make a difference.

As described in Chapter 2, three practices that encourage simplicity are *prioritize, tell stories*, and *keep messages simple*. Often in leadership improvement efforts coaches see many things that leaders could improve or training sessions offer dozens of ideas for improvement. By emphasizing improvements that can be implemented quickly and those which are lead indicators of other outcomes, leaders can prioritize what to change.

As you tell personal stories about the priorities you choose, they become less abstract and more tailored. Customized stories increase personal commitment. As these simple priorities and stories are repeated, they help you create and bring to life a new narrative about who you are as a leader. At the end of any coaching, performance review, or training session, take the time to winnow down the options for improvement into a few targeted priorities and weave these priorities into new outcomes that replace old patterns.

Here are some questions that help in the pursuit of simplicity:

- Of all the options I could take to improve, which are the two or three that I feel most inclined to start with?
  - Which ones do I think I could make quick progress on? Which ones are within my control?
  - Which ones am I confident I can make progress on?
  - Which ones are lead indicators of others?

- What are the stories I would like to tell about myself as a leader (and others to tell about me) when I make the improvements I prioritize? How will these stories create a new narrative about me as a leader?
- What simple message will I tell others about my areas for improvement? What common answers will I give to those who ask me what I can do to be a better leader?

These questions will help you to become a taxonomist for your own growth, prioritizing and sequencing changes that will have the most impact.

Step 4: How—Time

Key question: How do I manage my calendar to reflect my priorities to improve?

To do what you really want, you need to know what you're really doing. Chapter 4 invites leaders to be very conscious of how they manage their time, suggesting seven principles and practices to become a time logger. By following these ideas, you will manage your calendar rather than letting day-do-day demands manage you so that you and others will grow increasingly confident that promises will be fulfilled. Your calendar is a public commitment that signals what you believe matters most. To sustain change, do calendar management with discipline.

In our coaching, we often interview the leader's administrative assistant, the one who keeps the leader's calendar. We like to ask the administrative assistant to tell us the messages embedded in the leader's calendar. We also like to ask the administrative assistant to validate the leader's ability to match desired improvements with time (or reveal the gaps). In some cases, we encourage the leader to have regular and scheduled meetings with the administrative assistant for calendar checkups, and we even sit in as necessary.

As you manage your time, others will begin to see and respond to new behaviors—which tend to become habits. And as you announce these new habits with other signals (e.g., attire, space, and grooming), the habits become routines. These consistent routines endure over time, allowing you to change your identity.

Here are some questions that diagnose and facilitate the process of becoming a time logger:

- In the last day and week, what does my calendar say about me as a leader?
- Given what I would like to be known for, how would my calendar change to reflect that reputation?
  o Who would I meet with?
  o Where would I meet?
  o What issues would I spend more time on? Less time?
- What other symbolic changes could I make to demonstrate my desired reputation?

By answering these questions, you can become a time logger, recognizing time as your most critical resource and consciously attending to it to sustain improvements.

Step 5: How—Accountability

Key question: How do I make sure that I am personally and publicly accountable for making my improvements last?

Sustainable leaders are responsible adults who take personal responsibility for their past and future behaviors. It is easy and often natural to make excuses by blaming circumstances or others when desired changes are not sustained. For example, Dave tends to gain weight and likes to blame travel and airline food for his increasing girth. This is much more palatable than the thought that it might indicate a lack of personal discipline, respect for his body, or emotional control.

Personal honesty often serves as a litmus test of someone's ability to sustain change. A leader we coached kept running into the same problem—that of not making his people feel better about themselves. When we tried to coach him on his leadership, he kept deflecting the discussion to the issues with members of his team. He was adept at focusing on their weaknesses. He had insight into others but resisted the idea of facing his inability to build team unity. Over time, however, as we continued to focus him on his role in his team's performance and he learned to observe himself, he eventually accepted accountability for his role in team dynamics, and the team began to focus on its work rather than on his style. Leaders who are accountable face their problems and don't run away from them. They go public with their commitments, successes, and failures. They create a personal brand tied to the reputation they hope to achieve. When you become accountable, you are more likely to sustain change.

Answering the following questions will help to ensure that you act as a responsible adult:

- What is it about my behavior that causes the problems I keep facing?
- In my personal reflections, what do I know I need to change to be more effective? Who do I need to share this with?
- What do I need to apologize about? Who do I need to apologize to?
- What is my desired personal leadership brand? Is this personal brand consistent with my behavior?
- How public am I willing to be with the personal brand I hope to model? If people disagree with me, either because they don't agree with my desired brand or because I don't live up to it, will I listen to their comments without being defensive?

As you face the consequences of your choices, you become account-able to yourself and to others. This public and private accountability will help you to sustain change.

Step 6: How—Resources

Key question: How do I get the coaching and institutional support I need to be a better leader?

Leadership really is a team sport. You cannot lead in isolation, and you are unlikely to sustain your leadership improvements on your own. Being a good leader is like being a good teammate—someone who listens to others, who learns to work with others, and who respects the infrastructure that reinforces change.

We suggest two critical resources for sustaining change: coaching and infrastructure. Coaching means that leaders who intend to change will be more successful when they have a personal coach either inside or outside the company. Good coaches help leaders to recognize and change behaviors so that desired results follow. Sometimes friends can act as informal coaches, but other times it's desirable to engage someone with unique expertise and a defined role in guiding leaders. Broadway shows are better with good directors who coach actors on their roles; sports players work better as a team with a competent coach. Before ending a performance discussion, it helps to ask the leader being reviewed who will coach the changes.

With the right infrastructure, leaders' desired behaviors become woven into the fabric of the organization's governance. If leaders attempt a new behavior that is not rewarded, tied to promotion, or encouraged through communications, pursuing it will be a constant uphill fight. When you want to sustain change, look for ways to work with your HR colleagues who can weave desired improvements into HR practices. Before ending a performance discussion as either reviewer or subject, make sure that desired improvements become woven into training, compensation, communications, and career-development initiatives.

To discover resources to be a better teammate, consider the following questions:

- Who can I turn to for counsel as I try to make change?
  - Are there friends or peers who will serve as internal coaches to help me do what I intend?
  - Can I contract for expert coaching with someone who will work with me to accomplish my change?
- How do I institutionalize my desired behaviors into HR practices within my organization?
  - How can I make sure that my desired improvements are part of my formal performance appraisal? Rewards? Promotion or career opportunities?
- How do I work with others to make my changes meaningful to them?

As you weave these questions into leadership improvement dialogues, you will find that you are not left alone in your work to improve.

Step 7: How—Tracking

Key question: How do I make sure that I monitor my progress now and in the future?

Imagine saying such things as, "I will work harder," "I will listen better," and "I will change faster." These nice-to-do sentiments sound noble, but they will not sustain your efforts to be a better leader. By contrast, the four practices identified in Chapter 6 really help you to track your progress. When you have specific goals about how to measure your progress and then measure those goals regularly, share the information about those goals broadly, and have consequences tied to meeting or missing those goals, you'll find that the goals come into reach.

At the end of most of our leadership training workshops, we ask participants to write down simple and specific things that they will do, put this behavior into their calendar as soon as they get back to it, take personal ownership for the change, and resource the new behavior. But we also ask them to define specific measures that will let them know they have been successful. These metrics need to be about both behaviors and outcomes, short and long term. We often ask participants to share their intended metrics with a small cohort so that they can get reactions to the rigor of their metrics.

As you seek to build measures that enable tracking, consider the following questions:

- How will I know that I have been successful in making my desired improvements?
  - What will I do more of that others will be able to observe about me?
  - What will I do less of that others will be able to observe about me?
- What are the few critical measures that I will track to monitor my progress?
  - When will I collect them?
  - How will I collect them?
  - Who will I share them with?
- What is the consequence if I meet these measures? What is the consequence if I miss these measures?

As you answer these questions for yourself and others, you will track and almost certainly promote the progress of your desired improvements.

Step 8: How—Melioration

Key question: How do I constantly improve by learning, being resilient, and growing?

Change is not a linear dash (or trudge) from point *A* to point *B*. Instead, leaders who sustain desired improvements are like pioneers or jazz improvisers who constantly experiment, reflect, and improvise and who are resilient enough to adapt their behavior on the fly. These four practices will help you to learn from both successes and failures and enable you to grow into a new position. It is useful to work at constantly improving how well you sustain your commitment to sustainability.

In our coaching sessions, we often ask leaders to reflect on what they did since the previous coaching session. Rather than judge what they did or did not do, we ask them what they learned and how their experiences allow them to improve. Failing to sustain a personal change in the short term is not a crisis—as long as you face and improve from the experience. We often build our training sessions around learning solutions, where we ask leaders to share a problem or challenge they are facing, and then we offer them some new insights into how to solve the problem. We ask leaders to explicitly share what they learned about how they approached the problem before and after the training session.

To help someone meliorate, or to be a pioneer, we like to ask the following questions:

- In your recent efforts to improve your targeted behaviors, what worked well? Why?
- In your recent efforts to improve your targeted behaviors, what did not work? Why not?
- In the last 90 days, what have you learned about yourself as a leader?
- How do you approach failure? What questions do you ask to show that you are a learner?

- What do you do when things don't go well? How do you find resilience to go forward?

These questions will help you to go forward with confidence that you don't have to be perfect to make progress.

Step 9: How—Emotion

Key question: How do I find personal passion and meaning in my improvement efforts?

When you lead with heart as well as mind and body, you will find more success in sustaining change. To develop personal passion to sustaining your chosen change, recognize these principles and practices: finding personal passion in being a leader, constantly building personal energy, connecting improvements with personal values, connecting improvements with the organization's purpose, and recognizing the impact of personal improvements on others.

Often in professional settings people feel that they must abandon their personal passions. However, when leaders bring their personal passions to their desired improvements, they are more likely to sustain those changes. Through symbols, language, metaphors, or experiences, you can enhance your efforts to sustain change. One leader we coached to listen better told her team that she had shared her professional goals of listening with her teenage children. With some trepidation, her children responded by informing her that her listening challenges were present not only at work but also at home. As she talked more openly to her children and listened to their reflections and thoughts, she had an emotional connection as a parent with her children. She shared this personal experience at work and found some of the same emotion as she pledged to listen better both at home and at work.

Building emotion into your leadership improvements comes from raising questions such as:

- Why do I want to lead?
- What energizes or motivates me?
- How are my desired leadership improvements consistent with my broader life values?
- How will my desired leadership improvements help the organization reach its purpose?
- How will my desired leadership improvements help people I care about?

Pondering these questions will help you to find a reservoir of emotional strength as you try to sustain your changes.

Responsibility for Building Leadership Sustainability

As we've said, the challenge of leadership sustainability confronts each individual leader, and it also confronts leaders of others, those charged with building leaders (e.g., HR professionals), and the coaches or other external advisors who find their niche in improving organizational structures, activities, and processes. Those in each of these stakeholder groups who master the disciplines and principles not only become leaders who sustain change, but they also build it into their organizations.

Leader of Self

Ultimately, responsibility for being a sustainable leader rests with each individual. Every good leader wants to be better, but lasting improvement is hard to achieve. It requires knowing why improvement matters and what better leadership means, but it also requires knowing how to sustain what you start—and actually doing it.

Part of the role of leadership is modeling what others should do. Leaders lead from the front. They model what they want to see in others. We were in a company where the senior leaders wanted others to do a leadership 360-degree feedback session and have annual performance reviews but felt that they were immune from the need for similar experiences. We challenged, cajoled, and finally convinced them that they had to model the process of change for others. When these leaders went through the nine steps of the Leadership Sustainability Application Tool, they helped those they led see that they were serious about their personal change. As a result, others followed suit.

Leaders who take personal responsibility to sustain their leadership improvements constantly ask the *why, what,* and *how* questions. They recognize that leadership matters, that success as a leader requires doing the right things, and that leadership has to show up in actions more than in rhetoric. Such leaders earn the allegiance of their people, have their trust, and gain their best efforts.

Leader of Others

Leaders do not lead without followers. Followers gain confidence in their leaders when their leaders do what they promise. Leaders who help others to fulfill their leadership potential ensure that sustainability is not an isolated event but a shared responsibility. We like to talk about leadership capability being more important than individual leaders. Leaders build capability when they answer the *why, what,* and *how* questions for others.

To build leadership capability in an organization, leaders need to share why leadership matters. They also need to help every leader take personal responsibility to improve. They need to help leaders define what effective leadership means. Leaders of others also have to weave leadership sustainability into the fabric of the organization. They do so by making leadership sustainability part of the organization's leadership capability.

For eight years we have participated with Aon/Hewitt and *Fortune* magazine in identifying the top companies for leadership throughout the world. (In the last round of data collection in 2011, more than 450 firms provided input on their leadership practices.) Through rigorous selection criteria, the top 25 companies in the world for leadership are selected. We are then able to compare the leadership practices of the top 25 companies with those of the other 425. Many of these organization practices highlight sustainability. Table 9.1 summarizes the way many organization practices differentiate top companies for leadership.

Leaders of others should use the data in Table 9.1 to identify areas where they need to focus to build leadership sustainability as a part of the leadership capability. Top companies for leaders or those which have a reputation for leadership sustainability seriously invest in a host of leadership practices. These top companies for leadership sustainability invest more aggressively in recruiting, promoting, assessing, paying, developing, and tracking their leadership efforts. These efforts are what bring them a positive reputation for leadership sustainability.

Leaders of others need to recognize and invest in leadership sustainability practices and not shirk from their accountability for building future leaders. They should make leadership sustainability one of their priorities, dedicating their time to making it happen and being personally and publicly accountable for leadership sustainability. They also should provide resources for helping others to grow and metrics to track leadership progress. They should constantly be improving and growing, and they should bring personal passion to the development of leadership. In other words, leaders of others build leadership sustainability by applying the seven disciplines of START ME.

Table 9.1 Sustainability Practices of Top Companies for Leadership

Practice for Sustainability	Question	Top Companies	Other Companies
Recruiting leaders	Educating and developing leaders	100%	77%
	Identifying high-potential prospects	100%	81%
	Selecting leaders from within the company	96%	82%
	Recruiting leaders from outside the company	88%	65%
Managing high potentials	We formally identify high potentials or equivalents.	96%	72%
Succession planning	A specific CEO succession plan is in place.	100%	65%
	We have a formal succession planning process.	100%	72%
	We currently have a talent pipeline for CEOs.	88%	53%
	We currently have a talent pipeline for senior management.	92%	56%
	We currently have a talent pipeline for middle management.	88%	60%
	We currently have a talent pipeline for front-line management.	80%	58%
Assessment	Does your organization regularly use *360-degree feedback* (at least 80 percent of the time) to assess leaders for development?	88%	61%
	360-degree feedback for development	88%	68%
	360-degree feedback for performance management	60%	47%
	Does your organization regularly use *behavioral interviews* (at least 80 percent of the time) to assess leaders for development?	72%	45%

(Continued)

Table 9.1 Sustainability Practices of Top Companies for Leadership (Continued)

Practice for Sustainability	Question	Top Companies	Other Companies
Compensation	Does your organization hold leaders accountable, through compensation, for developing their direct reports?	88%	38%
	Does your organization clearly differentiate pay based on (check only one)		
	• Performance only	20%	46%
	• Performance and potential	80%	45%
Development	We have formal processes to develop senior management.	100%	74%
	We have formal processes to develop middle management.	100%	81%
	We have formal processes to develop front-line management.	100%	78%
	We have formal processes to develop high potentials.	100%	65%
	Do leaders regularly receive customized leadership training?	100%	76%
	Do leaders regularly participate as leaders as teachers?	88%	41%
	Do leaders regularly have external perspectives (customer needs, analyst reports) in the classroom?	76%	26%

Practice for Sustainability	Question	Top Companies	Other Companies
Measurement of leadership development	Does your organization use specific metrics to evaluate the effectiveness of your leadership development process?	92%	61%
	Does your organization use specific metrics to evaluate the effectiveness of your succession management process?	100%	48%
	Does your organization use specific metrics to evaluate the effectiveness of your high-potential (or equivalent) program?	84%	49%
External reputation for leadership	Does your organization intentionally build a reputation for strong leadership?	100%	66%
	We systematically communicate with internal and external stakeholders about our leadership investments and how they impact business results.	88%	61%
	We target communication with key customers.	80%	69%
	We target communication with investors.	72%	52%

HR Professionals

The broad umbrella of HR professionals include individuals charged with developing leadership within their company. These professionals have various titles: talent manager, learning officer, workforce planner, human capital developer, trainer, coach, human resources planner, leadership developer, and so forth. In our research, the variety and prominence of their roles have increased dramatically in the last 25 years. We consider the range of HR professionals to be architects for the *why, what,* and *how* questions. As architects, they should build blueprints or frameworks for building leadership that line managers—the owners—can use in their quest for sustainability.

We have worked with HR professionals for decades, helping them to define why leadership matters and what effective leadership looks like. Recently, we have come to believe that training, development, coaching, performance management, and other leadership improvement efforts are only a part of leadership improvement. We now strongly encourage this group of dedicated professionals to pay increased attention to the *how* of leadership by mastering and applying the 7 disciplines and 31 principles. When these insights become part of a leadership sustainability effort each initiative to improve leadership increases its impact for both personal leader improvement and organization leadership capability improvement.

Coaches or Other External Advisors

Wise leaders and HR professionals recognize that good ideas can come from both inside and outside the company. Using external coaches, consultants, or other advisors gives the organization access to innovative insights. Often consultants are valued for their ideas about why leadership matters. They help to create a case for investing in leadership. They help senior leaders to recognize the importance of leadership for employee productivity, customer share, investor market value, and community reputation. External advisors also can be very helpful in defining what makes an effective leader by sharing applicable research and practice from other companies. They can help to define competencies and to assess them with objective tests.

Too often external advisors end their work after building the case for leadership and defining what effective leadership looks like. We would suggest that organizations contract with external advisors to add more value in the leadership sustainability space. For true effectiveness, externally sponsored programs in training, coaching, or development need a significant component dedicated to leadership sustainability. External consultants, coaches, and advisors should be accountable not just for the design of ideas but also for the sustainable delivery of them.

Sometimes those who purchase external consulting services believe that the *why* and *what* questions are sufficient and that the *how* will take care of itself. We disagree. We believe that every external contract should be tied to implementation of insights.

Conclusion: Time to Soar

We began the work that led to this book with thousands of leaders with great aspirations to improve and commitment to do so. Most of them recognized that their abilities as a leader created value for stakeholders they cared about. They knew that leadership mattered and that they were important as leaders. Most of these leaders invested enormous personal commitment into improving. They studied books, attended seminars, took training seriously, prepared individual development plans, participated in leadership 360-degree sessions, received coaching, made career plans, and attended performance reviews. They were mostly committed to improving and were aware of what they needed to do to improve. But even as we congratulated ourselves on our leadership development efforts, we started to realize that the noble aspirations were not being fulfilled. Many of the leaders we worked with would meekly report that they had not implemented the improvements they intended. As we delved into these experiences, we realized that we were not alone. Much of the research on leadership implementation showed that leaders did not implement what they intended.

Like the poor studious birds whose story opens Chapter 1, after all that training to fly, they all walked home. So rather than pretend that this leadership challenge did not exist, we faced it squarely. We studied outstanding literatures on change, implementation, habits, and leadership derailment. We synthesized what we learned and experimented with the ideas in our leadership development work.

Finally, we synthesized the work of others and our own experiences into the STARTME mnemonic, capturing 7 disciplines and 31 principles of leadership sustainability. Leaders who apply these insights will make leadership last. They will deliver what they promise, and their leadership will endure.

We end this book with a challenge and a promise. We challenge you to not just read but also ponder, internalize, and apply these seven disciplines. We promise that if you do so, your leadership will move from rhetoric to results. Your personal brand will be about getting things done, and your leadership desires will be realized.

We encourage you to spread your wings and use the ideas presented here (and online at www.leadershipsustainability.com) and share your experiences with us.

iphone: **RedLaser**
Android: **Barcode Scanner**

Scan this QR code to download the STARTME app.

leadershipsustainability.com/qr/app

NOTES

Chapter 1

1. *Training Magazine* does an annual industry report in which the magazine shares trends in the industry. See www.trainingmag.com/article/2011-training-industry-report.
2. Bersin & Associates does an annual study of learning and development and spending trends. In 2010, its information was based on a survey of 748 U.S. organizations. The report is available at www.bersin.com. More can be read at Supervisory Management Training at eHow.com: www.ehow.com/about_4708246_supervisory-management-training.html#ixzz1EnGCMjOY.
3. The 10 percent knowledge transfer is reported in training magazines ("The Low-Hanging Fruit Is Tasty," *Chief Learning Officer*, March 2006), books (*The Learning Alliance*, by Robert Brinkerhoff and Stephen Gill). See also T. T. Baldwin and J. K. Ford, "Transfer of Training: A Review and Directions for Future Research," *Personnel Psychology* 41:63–105, 1988; and D. L. Georgenson, "*The Problem of Transfer Calls for Partnership*," *Training & Development Journal* 36(10):75, 1982.
4. A. M. Saks and M. Belcourt, "An Investigation of Training Activities and Transfer of Training in Organizations," *Human Resource Management* 45(4):629–648, 2006.
5. Duke Executive Leadership Survey, 2009.
6. Robert Gandossy and Marc Effron, *Leading the Way: Three Truths from the Top Companies for Leaders* (New York: Wiley, 2003); available at: www.aon.com/human-capital-consulting/thought-leadership/leadership/reports-pub_top_companies.jsp. See also Erin Burns, Laurence Smith, and Dave Ulrich, "Competency

Models with Impact: Research Findings from the Top Companies for Leaders," *People and Strategy*, Vol. 35, Issue 3 pp. 16-23, 60.

7. Katharina Herrmann, Asmus Komm, and Sven Smit, "Do You Have the Right Leaders for Your Growth Strategy? *McKinsey Quarterly*, July 2011.

8. *Creating People Advantage 2011* (Boston: Boston Consulting Group, 2011).

9. The names of the individuals we refer to have been changed to provide anonymity.

10. Kerry Patterson, Joseph Grenny, David Maxfield, Ron McMillan, and Al Switzler, *Change Anything: The New Science of Personal Success* (New York: Business Plus, 2011).

11. These generous thought leaders included Jim Bolt (working on leadership development efforts), Richard Boyatzis (working on the competency models and resonant leadership), Jay Conger (working on leadership skills as aligned with strategy), Bob Fulmer (working on leadership skills), Bob Eichinger (working with Mike Lombardo to extend work from the Center for Creative Leadership on leadership abilities), Marc Effron (working on large studies of global leaders), Marshall Goldsmith (working on global leadership skills and how to develop those skills), Gary Hamel (working on leadership as it relates to strategy), Linda Hill (working on how managers become leaders and leadership in emerging economies), Jon Katzenbach (working on leaders from within the organization), Jim Kouzes (working on how leaders build credibility), Morgan McCall (representing the Center for Creative Leadership), Barry Posner (working on how leaders build credibility), Jack Zenger and Joe Folkman (working on how leaders deliver results and become extraordinary), Jon Younger (who writes, talks, and designs intellectual property around our human resources practice), and Bob Gandossy (who has run the "Top Companies for Leaders" study that we cosponsor with Aon Hewitt and *Fortune* magazine every two years).

Chapter 2

1. Charles Duhigg, *The Power of Habit: Why We Do What We Do in Life and Business* (New York: Random House, 2012).
2. www.elliott.org/blog/southwest-airlines-pilot-holds-plane-for-murder-victims-family/.

Chapter 3

1. International Bureau of Weights and Measures, *The International System of Units (SI)*, 8th ed. (2006). ISBN 92-822-2213-6. See http://www.bipm.org/utils/common/pdf/si_brochure_8_en.pdf.
2. Stephen Hawking and Leonard Mlodinow, *A Briefer History of Time* (New York: Bantam, 2008); Paul Davies, *About Time: Einstein's Unfinished Revolution* (New York: Simon & Shuster, 1996).
3. Henry Mintzberg, *Nature of Managerial Work* (New York: Prentice-Hall, 1980).
4. Ron Heifetz and Donald Laurie, "The Work of Leadership," *Harvard Business Review*, January–February 1997.
5. Chester Barnard, *Functions of the Executive* (Cambridge, MA: Harvard University Press, 1956).
6. James Claiborn and Cherry Pedrick, *The Habit Change Workbook: How to Break Bad Habits and Form Good Ones.* (Oakland, California: New Harbinger Publications, 2001).
7. Dave Ulrich, Ron Ashkenas, and Steve Kerr, *The GE Work-Out* (San Francisco: Jossey-Bass, 2002).
8. Christy A. Visher, "Transitions from Prison to Community: Understanding Individual Pathways." The Urban Institute, Justice Policy Center, Washington, DC, 2003.
9. "Bureau of Justice Statistics Recidivism of Prisoners Released in 1994"; available at: Ojp.usdoj.gov; retrieved September 14, 2009.
10. National Institute on Drug Abuse (NIDA), *National Survey on Drug Use and Health (NSDUH).* (Washington, DC: NIDA, 2006).

11. http://en.wikipedia.org/wiki/Seat_belt_use_rates_in_the_USA.

12. Maxwell Maltz, *Psycho-Cybernetics: A New Way to Get More Living Out of Life* (New York: Prentice-Hall, 1960).

Chapter 4

1. Jack Schenker, "Mubarak on Trial: Middle East Live," *Guardian*, August 3, 2011.

2. Linda Galindo, *The 85% Solution* (San Francisco: Jossey-Bass, 2009), p. 25.

3. Anthony K. Tjan, "Why Some People Have All the Luck," HBR Blog, July 6, 2011. http://blogs.hbr.org/tjan/2011/07/why-some-people-have-all-the-l.html.

Chapter 5

1. An overview of the social network village for retired individuals can be found in Martha Thomas, "The Real Social Network," *AARP: The Magazine*, April 2011.

2. The concepts on measures and rewards are drawn from Edward E. Lawler, *Strategic Pay: Aligning Organizational Strategies and Pay Systems* (San Francisco: Jossey-Bass, 1990); and Steve Kerr, "Some Characteristics and Consequences of Organizational Rewards," in F. David Schoorman and Benjamin Schneider (eds.), *Facilitating Work Effectiveness* (Lexington, MA: Lexington Books, 1988). See also Geoffrey Colvin, "The Great CEO Pay Heist," *Fortune*, June 25, 2001, p. 64; and Alfred Rappaport (ed.), *Harvard Business Review on Compensation* (Boston: Harvard Business School Press, 2002).

3. Jay R. Galbraith, *Designing Complex Organizations* (Reading, MA: Addison-Wesley, 1973).

Chapter 6

1. *New York Times*, February 2, 2012; Magazine, shopping habits; www.nytimes.com/2012/02/19/magazine/shopping-habits. html?pagewanted=1&_r=2.

2. *Forbes*, February 16, 2012, http://www.forbes.com/sites/kashmir-hill/2012/02/16/how-target-figured-out-a-teen-girl-was-pregnant-before-her-father-did/.

3. Lyle M. Spencer, Jr., *Calculating Human Resource Costs and Benefits* (New York: Wiley, 1986); and Lyle M. Spencer, Jr., *Competence at Work: Models for Superior Performance* (New York: Wiley, 1995).

4. Richard Hackman and Greg Oldman, *Work Redesign* (Reading, MA: Addison-Wesley, 1980); Greg Oldman and Richard Hackman, "How Job Characteristics Theory Happened," in K. G. Smith and M. A. Hitt (eds.), *The Oxford Handbook of Management Theory: The Process of Theory Development* (Oxford, UK: Oxford University Press, 2005), pp. 151–170.

5. Alfie Kohn, *Punished by Rewards: The Trouble with Gold Stars, Incentive Plans, A's, Praise, and Other Bribes* (Boston: Houghton Mifflin, 1999).

6. Bob Nelson, *1001 Ways to Reward Employees* (New York: Workman, 1994); Bob Nelson, *1001 Ways to Energize Employees* (New York: Workman, 1997).

Chapter 7

1. Henry Mintzberg, "The Manager's Job: Folklore and Fact," HBR July–August 1975; Thomas Peters and Robert Waterman, *In Search of Excellence* (New York: HarperBusiness, 1982).

2. R. E. Kaplan and R. B. Kaplan, *The Versatile Leader: Make the Most of Your Strengths—Without Overdoing It* (San Francisco: Pfeiffer, 2006).

3. Gene Dalton, Louis Barnes, and Abraham Zaleznik, *The Distribution of Authority in Formal Organizations* (Boston: Harvard Business School Press, 1968).

4. Edgar Schein, *A Socio-psychological Analysis of the "Brainwashing" of American Civilian Prisoners by the Chinese Communists* (New York: Norton, 1971).

5. Learning agility has recently been discussed in the following sources: Victoria Swisher, *Becoming an Agile Leader* (Minneapolis: Lominger International, 2012); Ken DeMeuse, Guangrong Dai, and George Hallenback, "Learning Agility: A Construct Whose Time Has Come," *Consulting Psychology Journal: Practice and Research* 62(2):119–130, June 2010; Michael Lombardo and Bob Eichinger, "High Potentials as High Learners," *Human Resource Management* 39:321–330, 2000; R. W. Eichinger and M. M. Lombardo, "Learning Agility as a Prime Indicator of Potential," *Human Resource Planning* 27(4):12–16, 2004; R. W. Eichinger, M. M. Lombardo, and C. C. Capretta, *FYI for Learning Agility* (Minneapolis: Lominger International, 2010).

6. Jeff Dyer, Hal Gregerson, and Clayton Christensen, *Innovators DNA* (Boston: Harvard Business School Press, 2011).

7. George Hallenbeck and Bob Eichinger, *Interviewing Right: How Science Can Sharper Your Interviewing Accuracy* (San Francisco: Korn Ferry, 2006).

8. M. J. Ryan, *This Year I Will . . . : How to Finally Change a Habit, Keep a Resolution, or Make a Dream Come True* (New York: Crown Archetype, 2006); Albert Ellis, *Overcoming Destructive Beliefs, Feelings, and Behaviors: New Directions for Rational Emotive Behavior Therapy* (New York: Prometheus Books, 2001).

9. Julia Cameron, *The Artists Way* [Los Angeles: Tarcher (Penguin), 2002].

10. Lee Perry, Randy Stott, and Norm Smallwood, *Real Time Strategy* (New York: Wiley, 1993). Others also have used the metaphor of

a jazz ensemble to demonstrate organization agility: Karl Weick, M. Bougon, and D. Binkhorst, "An Analysis of the Utrecht Jazz Orchestra," *Administrative Science Quarterly* 22:606–639, 1977; Max Depree, *Leadership Jazz: The Essential Elements of a Great Leader* (New York: Crown, 2008).

11. See www.nobelprize.org/nobel_prizes/medicine/laureates/1979/perspectives.html.

Chapter 8

1. A. Freitas-Magalhães, *The Psychology of Emotions: The Allure of Human Face* (Oporto, Portugal: University Fernando Pessoa Press, 2007); P. Ekman, "Basic Emotions," in T. Dalgleish and M. Power (eds.), *Handbook of Cognition and Emotion* (Sussex, UK: Wiley, 1999); J. E. LeDoux, "The Neurobiology of Emotion," in J. E. LeDoux and W. Hirst (eds.), *Mind and Brain: Dialogues in Cognitive Neuroscience* (New York: Cambridge University Press, 1986), Chap. 15; G. Mandler, *Mind and Body: Psychology of Emotion and Stress* (New York: Norton, 1984).

2. This statistic comes from a presentation by Kevin Roberts—CEO Saatchi and Saatchi.

3. There are many value lists that you can take for self-assessment. We would recommend: www.listofvalues.com/; www.mypersonal improvement.com/personalcorevalues.html; www.sustainable-employ ee-motivation.com/personal-values.html; and http://enspireme. org/wp-content/uploads/2011/11/Core-Values-Exercise.pdf.

4. www.skills21ead.com/sample-vision-statements.html.

5. Christopher Peterson and Martin Seligman, *Character Strengths and Virtues: A Handbook and Classification* (New York: Oxford University Press, 2004).

6. Martin Seligman, *Authentic Happiness: Using the New Positive Psychology to Realize Your Potential for Lasting Fulfillment* (New

York: Free Press, 2003); Martin Seligman, *Flourish: A Visionary New Understanding of Happiness and Well-Being* (New York: Free Press, 2012).

7. Jim Underwood, *More Than a Pink Cadillac: Mary Kay, Inc.'s Nine Leadership Keys to Success* (New York: McGraw-Hill, 2004).

Chapter 9

1. We should note that this Leadership Sustainability Application Tool is available for download or online at www.leadershipsustainability.com. The app is free with the purchase of this book.

INDEX

ABOUT THE AUTHORS

Dave Ulrich is a Professor at the Ross School of Business, University of Michigan and a partner at The RBL Group (http://www.rbl.net) a consulting firm focused on helping organizations and leaders deliver value. His insights have shaped how organizations build capabilities of leadership, speed, learning, accountability, and talent through leveraging human resources. He has helped generate award-winning data bases that assess alignment between strategies, organization capabilities, HR practices, HR competencies, and customer and investor results. He has published over 200 articles and book chapters and over 25 books. He has received numerous lifetime achievement awards and has been ranked number 1 most influential thinker in human resources for five of the last six years in Human Resource Management. He has consulted and done research with over half of the Fortune 200.

Norm Smallwood is a recognized authority in developing businesses and their leaders to deliver results and increase value.

His work focuses on collaborating with clients to build organization capabilities that align with strategic intent, develop leadership and talent to deliver results, and enable HR communities to make a more value added difference to their business.

In 2010, the *Harvard Business Review* recognized Norm in an ad for the magazine as doing "innovative and ground-breaking work on effective leadership."

Norm has coauthored several books: *Real-Time Strategy, Results-Based Leadership, How Leaders Build Value, Change Champions Field Guide, Leadership Brand,* and *Leadership Code.* He has published articles in leading journals and newspapers including *Washington Post, Forbes,* and *Financial Times* and has contributed chapters and

Forewords to multiple books. Norm has been a frequent blogger on HBR Online where his blog on Personal Leader Brand was highlighted as one of 10 most read of 2010.

For several years, *Leadership Excellence* magazine has ranked Norm as one of the top 100 Global Voices in Leadership and The RBL Group as one of the top leadership development firms in the world.

On the family side, Norm and his wife Tricia are the designated leaders of two Great Danes—Fritz and Freddy—along with a couple of cats—Max and Achilles—a school of koi (fish), and assorted children and grandchildren.